I, dea

Awaken Your Inner Goddess

Samantha Dreiling

ISBN: 979-8-6345-2810-6

To every woman who has ever forgotten her power.

CONTENTS

Conception

Noun
DEA *f* (*plural* dees) Latin
Goddess

At the end of 2019, looking into a new decade, I made a prayer and intention that in the following year, a book would flow through me. I had no idea what it would be about or when it would happen, but I asked that it be part of my soul work, with a message that would serve people. I've been doing this work in different ways for years but I could never figure out the direction in which I was meant to take it.

At sixteen years old, I was working as an assistant in a hair salon. I worked there for over three years. What I loved about the work was pampering people: after a long day, clients would come in and I would wash their hair and massage their scalps; I could feel their tension and stress melt away in my hands and wash down the drain. My clients, most of whom were women, felt deeply connected to me because I was in their personal bubble. I acted as a catalyst for them to open up. I helped remind these clients of the gorgeous goddess deep within them, and our connection allowed them to feel the way they always should: pampered and beautiful.

Through this powerful connection, I felt aligned with the work, but the environment was very toxic. The salon was owned and run by a man who led with a traditional patriarchal, domineering mindset, which was certainly *not* in alignment with the almost spiritual service I felt we were providing our clients. After three years of hard work

9

sweeping the floors, cleaning brushes and bowls, and washing hundreds of heads, he didn't even call me by my name. When he needed my help, he would snap his fingers and say, "Hey, lady!" and I was expected to come running like his servant.

I remember one evening, after a hard day's work, he pulled me into a meeting where he told the staff that "time was money" and that we were "here on *his* time to make *his* salon money." He ended the meeting by saying, "You are all replaceable." After he spoke, I looked around the room and saw all the passion and self-worth drain from the faces of the women around me. Unsurprisingly, their feelings of subjugation and disrespect were quickly replaced by rage and indignation, and not long after that meeting, nearly half of the women left to work elsewhere.

This was a prime example of Divine Feminine power being overtaken and quashed by the human masculine desire for money and control. It was painful for my soul, and I decided I could no longer participate in that poisonous dynamic.

I left that job and became a freelance makeup artist to continue cultivating the joy I received from empowering and pampering women. For me, makeup was (and still is!) about taking the beautiful canvas of a woman and bringing her divine inner beauty to the surface.

Too often, barefaced and feeling vulnerable, these gorgeous goddesses would feel the need to apologize for their "imperfections." They'd say things like, "Sorry I have really dark circles" or "Sorry about my big nose." I'd hear strong, stunning women apologize for their "hooded eyes" or their "terrible skin." It broke my heart. Why do we women feel this need to apologize for our bodies? Why do we believe our beauty is only skin deep?

Many times, after I finished my art, my clients would look in the mirror and tear up, saying, "I didn't know I could look so beautiful." Sometimes for the very first time, they felt seen by someone else at a deeper level. A light within them was reawakened after becoming acquainted with the goddess they saw staring back at them from the mirror.

These magical moments presented me with an opportunity to breathe life into women; to remind them that their beauty went so much deeper. I would tell them, "Your beauty comes from within, and when you take time to pamper and treat yourself, it can shine. It was always there; you just needed a reminder to notice it." My clients would thank me, hug me, and then often share their deeper insecurities with me. This intimate connection of touching their faces and exploring their beauty—and their perceived "flaws"—required them to let down their walls and be truly seen.

As a freelance makeup artist, I built an incredible client base of female entrepreneurs, authors, models, brides, and actresses. I worked on photoshoots for magazines and did creative collaborations with amazing photographers who became great friends. When an opportunity arose to open a branch of a private makeup academy, my intuition told me it would be the perfect platform to teach others how to cultivate their own passion for making people feel beautiful.

I loved watching my students fulfill their dreams by becoming makeup artists, and was inspired by the diversity among them. The academy attracted students from all walks of life and a wide range of ages: some students were as young as fifteen years old, hungry and eager to follow their passion; others were in their twenties or thirties, dabbling with a new career; and then there were awe-inspiring women over sixty, who were finally choosing to push their fears aside and pursue their long-dormant dreams. What all these women had in common was their desire to make others feel good through the power of makeup artistry, and I was devoted to helping them.

Alongside teaching the techniques of applying makeup, I learned that many, if not most, of the women needed direction both in their businesses and their self-belief. It became my mission to remind them that not only were they beautiful and powerful, but they were also worthy of a successful career they loved. I wanted to teach them they could do something they were passionate about *and* create financial abundance from it. Owning and operating the academy helped me find an even deeper passion for helping women believe in themselves and guiding them on how to share their unique gifts with the world. For the next four years, I watched the Divine Feminine take over my students with creativity, power, and confidence.

Around the same time, I joined a health and wellness company that was on a mission to empower people to use clean, healthy products as well as build their own businesses. I felt empowered to be working with a company whose core values were helping people and the planet, while also prioritizing ethical business practices over profit. Even though I didn't think I was good at sales, I believed in the mission and the products so much that I passionately shared them with everyone anyway. And using the makeup products on my clients felt in alignment with my higher values because I was offering pure, beneficial products, free of harsh and harmful chemicals, that actually provided results.

Through using these incredible products and learning more about the importance of safe ingredients, I began to see my body as a temple for the goddess within. Caring for that temple with clean, pure products and healthy, vibrant foods was transformative for me. What had started as a simple desire to use cleaner products soon turned into a passion for helping my fellow humans, particularly women, awaken and start living life on purpose.

Once again, I found myself deeply connected to women and on a mission to remind them of their power within. Fulfillment exploded within me when someone I was working with would step into their power and get excited about whom they could serve and what they could create. The community I found and built through this company would continue to change my life over the next decade.

My health and wellness business reflected back to me where I needed to grow and what I needed to learn in order to move forward. Every single obstacle I had to overcome was an opportunity for growth; a lesson that elevated me to the next version of myself.

As I continued to evolve spiritually, a soul sister and I began facilitating goddess circles where we worked deeply with women to reconnect to their divine power and honor their monthly cycles. Women came together ready to transform and learn how to love themselves and their bodies. We focused on changing the association with our cycles from an annoying, painful experience to a gift of transcendence and growth. I knew within my heart and soul this was something I was meant to share; throughout this book we will delve into many of the teachings and topics these goddesses and I explored, as well as new discoveries I have since made.

All of these experiences have connected me to my life's purpose, and now my work flows almost effortlessly, with the guidance of the Divine Feminine. Just days after setting the intention to write a book, I was kept awake at night with swarms of ideas. I kept pondering the word "goddess," returning over and over again to my mission of awakening the Divine within millions of souls on this earth. One night, again unable to sleep due to Divine Inspiration, I picked up my phone and started researching. Eventually, I came across the Latin word for goddess: *Dea*. It was so beautiful; so simple. I started saying to myself, "*Dea, Dea, Dea* . . . idea . . . I . . . *DEA*. I, *Dea!*" I, the Divine Goddess. I, as in YOU. *Dea*, as in the Divine Feminine power living within you, yearning to come out. My work, my mission, my message . . . what an *Idea*. Like puzzle pieces coming together, I could now see the whole picture. I felt determined to change the limited notions we have about ourselves. I felt called to show women how they too could claim "I, *Dea!*" and knowingly shout from the depths of their Divine Feminine, "I am powerful beyond measure, guided by the Divine, and I am capable of anything I desire!"

My soul knew the message I had to share, and the following pages are filled with story after story from my own journey. These stories are not ones I would usually share publicly, but I must. Not everyone is ready for these messages, not everyone will relate, but for those who are ready and are meant to receive them, I call you in now.

Your inner goddess guided you to this book. She has spoken clearly and the message is clear: it is time to awaken. It is time to claim Her as YOU. To work alongside Her, and call upon Her for guidance and help. To remember who you truly are. To wake up from the patriarchal, power-driven nightmare we have endured for thousands of years. It is our duty to step back into our true, innate, Divine essences, and shine our lights, which have been dimmed too long.

The journey will not always be easy. There is deep work to be done. Patterns and beliefs—beliefs that have been deeply rooted for so long even we have started to believe we are limited—must be turned around, re-programmed, and transformed. Society has conditioned us to believe we must look, act, think, and feel a certain way. No more. We are here to break the mold. We are caterpillars now, but as we go inward and awaken the *Dea* from her slumber, we will inevitably break free of our cocoons, transformed into majestic, beautiful butterflies.

If you are ready to embark on the journey, turn the page and let's begin.

Chapter 1

When We First Met

In the summer of 2010, I was living in Toronto, where I was preparing to take a makeup artistry course. I was four hours from my hometown of Ottawa, and even though I was excited for the makeup course and exploring the big city, I missed my family. Luckily, my grandparents and beloved aunt lived just an hour outside of Toronto and on one sunny day in July, my aunt invited me to visit her in the countryside. I decided to take the train out of the big city to visit for a few days before my classes started.

As a little girl, I'd always loved spending time with my aunt; in fact, some of my fondest memories from childhood were of her teaching me how to ride horses. By the time I accepted her invitation to visit that July, however, it had been about ten years since I'd sat upon a horse.

The morning after I arrived, my aunt drove us from her house to the barn where she kept her horses. As we cruised through rural Ontario, I felt myself reconnecting with a part of myself I hadn't realized I'd lost. I gazed out the window, taking in the majesty of a blissful summer day, noticing how the sun's rays touched every blade of verdant grass in fields that stretched as far as my eyes could see. The sky was electric blue, with white, billowy clouds peppered throughout. I simultaneously felt so small, and yet so . . . *powerful*. I felt connected to it all.

As we got closer to the barn, I started to get nervous, but excited, about riding again. I couldn't wait to reconnect with these beautiful animals, and hoped the experience would be as freeing and wonderful as I remembered. When we arrived, we were greeted by my aunt's friend, and the three of us went straight to the barn. My aunt suggested I ride her calm, older gelding. Since I was out of practice, I was happy to oblige and looked forward to a slow, peaceful jaunt. The three of us, now saddled up and atop our horses, walked out the barn doors to the sandy arena, and began to trot. My sweet, gentle horse seemed to be enjoying himself, and I started to relax into the rhythm of the ride.

Within the fenced area there were different jumps and props for horses to use when practicing for shows. I had never jumped anything on a horse before so we carefully avoided them as we made our first few laps. Then suddenly, without any direction from me, my horse started to pick up speed, moving from a trot to a canter. I felt free and exhilarated as we flew around the ring. My aunt called out, "Look at you!" It had been years since I'd ridden, let alone go so fast, and though I was enjoying the ride, I wanted to slow down and catch my breath. When I tried to slow my horse down, however, he sped up! We were whipping around the arena in frantic, fast-paced circles, lapping my aunt and her friend over and over again. My aunt, who could feel my rising panic, called out directions for me to slow him down, but nothing I did worked. I'd totally lost control. My aunt and her friend, who were experienced riders, tried to slow down my horse and calm him, but that only seemed to make him gallop faster. My aunt looked horrified—she couldn't believe her sweet horse with a lame leg had taken off with her niece on his back!

I held on as tightly as I could, while my helmet—which was far too big for me—kept falling over my eyes. I tried to slow down my horse, but the reins kept slipping. I knew I needed to adjust my helmet so I could see, so I bravely removed one hand from the perilously slippery reins and shoved the helmet back—at which point, I discovered we were heading straight for a jump. My stomach clenched and I held on for dear life as we soared over it. Then, to make matters worse, my horse decided it had had enough of the arena, and decided to escape.

We galloped around the property, doing laps around the farmhouse and trees, with my aunt and her friend in hot pursuit. Those few minutes felt like an eternity, but eventually, I was able to steer us back towards the arena, where I plotted my own escape. As we were running full speed along the arena's fence, I tried to gauge where it would be safest to dismount. To my left was the arena fence, but I realized that if I fell on the fence, especially at that speed, I would probably break my back. To my right was sand, which didn't seem ideal but much safer than the other option. My horse was heading straight for an adjacent fence, and I could tell he was going to attempt another jump. I had to make a choice: ride the horse indefinitely until he lost steam; get bucked off backwards as he sailed over the fence; or jump. With all my might, I swung my left leg over and threw my body off the horse, into the sand.

My aunt and her friend caught up to me and dismounted, while my horse . . . stopped! He stood perfectly still, gazing back at me, looking surprised I'd had the audacity to abandon him on our great adventure together.

I had landed directly on my right hip. After a moment of assessing the damage, I thought I was fine, grateful I was alive and seemingly unscathed. My aunt asked me if I could stand but when I tried to move my legs, or any of my lower body at all, I realized I couldn't. It felt like my legs had detached from my body, as if I had no muscles at all. Both women lifted me by my arms and carried me to the car so my aunt could drive me to the emergency room.

I was in shock at first, but as the adrenaline wore off, the pain grew stronger. I kept trying to move my legs, but nothing happened. When we arrived at the hospital, I was put in a wheelchair and wheeled to the x-ray room. Hours later, a doctor explained I had torn pelvic muscles, as well as a hairline fracture across the bottom of my pelvic bone. He also said I'd be walking with crutches for months.

Even though the pain was by far the worst I had ever felt, I made an effort to smile through the whole ordeal. I was relieved and grateful my injuries were not worse, and felt blessed knowing I would make a full recovery.

Since I couldn't return to Ottawa right away, I stayed with my grandparents for a few days while we figured out what my recovery protocol would be. Every morning, my eighty-year-old grandfather would push me in my wheelchair through the nearby park, and every few minutes, he'd ask if I was alright. I assured him I was, but the truth was I felt more than alright; I was swimming in a sea of golden gratitude, more alive and awake to the world than ever. I had transformed from a self-conscious nineteen-year-old, who picked apart her weirdly shaped legs, ankles, and cellulite, to an empowered young woman who finally loved every inch and cell of her beautiful, powerful, healthy legs.

I marveled at how miraculously mind-blowing my legs were: they'd taken me on grand sight-seeing adventures;

allowed me to walk and run; and supported me while I danced, without a second thought. Prior to this incident it had never occurred to me I'd been taking my legs for granted, as opposed to worshipping their every amazing feat. This experience initiated a chain of events that would change me forever. I had awakened to a deeper meaning of life, and a profound gratitude and love for my body.

In spite of my newfound awe for my body, I was grappling with the doctors' prognosis: it would probably take me six months to walk properly again. While grateful I would walk again, my wonderful legs and I had a pretty special date I was not ready to miss: an incentive trip, which I'd earned through my health and wellness business, to the Atlantis Resort in the Bahamas. The trip was in three weeks, and I was determined to be there—*without* a wheelchair!

I thanked the local doctors for all they'd done to help me and urgently went home (now on crutches) to Ottawa, where I could see my acupuncturist. He was a doctor of Traditional Chinese Medicine—an incredible healer—who'd previously helped me with back and knee issues.

My mom took me to my appointment. When it was time to go into the private room, she had to help me down the hallway. Because of the severe tears in the muscles connecting my legs to my pelvis, my mobility was awkward and slow: I had to put both crutches ahead of me, then pick up one leg at a time and place it a step in front of me. Crutch-crutch, leg-leg. Crutch-crutch, leg-leg. It was tedious, but eventually we got to the room, my mom helped me up onto the exam table and returned to the waiting room, and I lied down on my left side. The doctor proceeded to place acupuncture needles throughout my back, legs, feet, and head. Before leaving the room, he pressed play on a little boom box. Meditative music lulled me into a deep, peaceful trance.

After about forty minutes I felt warm energy swirling through and around my body. I felt as though I was floating, like each individual cell was dancing. And then, though my eyes were closed, I saw Her.

She stood over me, swirling her hands up and down the length of my body, which caused the energy to multiply and intensify until I felt a profound sensation: I was healing. *She* was healing me. It felt so real, *She* looked so real, that I had to open my eyes and look around the room—I needed a tangible connection with this ethereal being. The room was empty and yet, I still felt Her nearby. I closed my eyes again and there she was, clear as day: she had long, wavy, auburn hair that flowed in all directions, unaffected by gravity, alive in a wind I couldn't feel; she wore a burnt orange-colored robe, that glowed like the embers of a thousand fires; and she was divinely, breath-takingly beautiful. I could feel her spirit too: wise, powerful, peaceful, and all-knowing.

This was my first gracious encounter with my *Dea*. The goddess. *My* goddess. The light and power within me was awakening.

My doctor returned to the room, removed the needles, and had me sit up. Then he asked me to stand. As I lifted each leg and swung them over the side of the table, I suddenly realized they weren't dead weight anymore and they no longer felt feeble and broken. As I put my weight onto my left leg, then my right, I could feel the strength of my muscles and the sturdiness of my bones in a way I hadn't since before I'd thrown myself from that horse. My doctor directed me to take a few steps, so I reached for my crutches.

"Without the crutches," he said. I looked at him like he was absolutely insane, positive my newfound wellness was a fluke.

"But I'll fall," I replied.

"Trust me. Just try," he said with encouragement.

I was still in a daze from my mystical experience, and couldn't find the words to argue with him, so I took a step. And then another. And yet another! My gait wasn't perfect, and ultimately, I still needed the crutches for stability, but I was *walking*. Not limping or having to hurl one leg in front of me every time I wanted to take a step. I made my way out of the room and down the hallway, toward the waiting area— where I found my very stunned looking mother, whose jaw was practically on the floor. At my two-week follow-up appointment, my western doctor was equally dumbfounded when I walked into her office without crutches.

Three weeks after the incident, after I'd been told it would be six months before I walked normally again, I found myself basking in the warm Atlantic Ocean off the coast of the Bahamas. I had made it on my trip, whole and well, with a newfound appreciation for my body. Over the course of my vacation, I couldn't stop thinking about the beautiful, divine goddess who'd helped me heal. For the very first time, I felt truly awake, as if I'd been reborn—body, mind, and soul. My trauma had been transformed into a life-altering triumph. It was my first time really experiencing a breakthrough after a breakdown. And it became my mission to become better acquainted with the *Dea* within me. I didn't want to lose her, and more importantly, I wanted to help other women awaken their inner goddesses.

Your *Dea* is waiting for you, desperate to come out of hiding, but She needs you to find Her. Like the genie in the lamp, you must bring Her to life.

I promise, you won't have to fall off a horse to call Her.

SOUL WORK

Visit AwakenDea.com for a complementary guided meditation that will help you discover your inner goddess. Your *Dea* is waiting to meet you!

Once you've completed the meditation, find a special notebook or journal and write down everything you remember about your experience, including what your *Dea* looked like. You can even draw her, if you feel inspired.

Keep this designated notebook with you as you read the rest of the book and complete more Soul Work!

Share your experience online with #IdeaSoulWork.

Chapter 2

Uncovering My Own Truth

There is a story:

A man was walking in the woods when suddenly he came upon a lovely tree. As he admired the tree, he spotted a beautiful, bright red creature. Enamored with the creature, he hurried home to tell a friend about it. After entertaining his friend with his tale, his friend remarked, "Oh yes! I too have seen that creature. But you are wrong in saying that it is red. It is, in fact, green " Overhearing their conversation, another friend approached the two men and argued, "You're both wrong! I have seen the creature and he is yellow!" The men could not agree, so they went into the woods to find the creature, each determined to prove his two friends wrong. As they approached the lovely tree, they noticed a small shelter, underneath which sat an old man. The three friends asked the old man if he had seen the creature, but they continued to argue over what color it was. In the midst of their heated exchange, the old man finally spoke. "My friends, you are all right, and you are all wrong, for this animal of which you speak is a Chameleon. He is also blue, black, and at times completely colorless. It is only the one who sees him at all times who knows of his true nature."[1]

This story draws a lovely parallel to the paradox of religion and spirituality. The chameleon represents God, and the different colors are representations of the various scriptures and teachings about God—all unique, but equally beautiful. Humanity has spent millennia arguing over which ideology is the absolute truth, but of course we can't all agree. One's relationship with God is deeply personal and manifests in different ways for different people. What if these differences were on purpose, to continually expand our consciousness and understanding of who or what is God? What if we're meant to believe different things, that are neither good nor bad, to challenge us to be more empathetic to one another? What if, instead of obsessing over who is right, fighting for one singular interpretation and belief system, we observed God in His/Her ever-changing perfection?

When I was young, my family went to church, usually only around Christmas and Easter. We attended Christian services because my mom had been raised Christian, but my family never really talked about our actual *beliefs*. We attended church out of obligation and ritual, not out of a need for connection to our faith (which was nebulous anyway). To confuse matters even more, my father was actually an atheist, and often expressed his belief that we are here without any true purpose. He believed we are born, we live, we die, and we return to the earth: the cycle of life, without any spiritual bells or whistles.

As children, I remember my sister and I being dragged to Sunday school, upset we'd had to wake up early. I was uncomfortable being there and couldn't get into the stories or teachings—it all felt off to me. Something just didn't resonate, and every time I was at church, I got a pit in my stomach. I wanted to believe in God, I wanted to believe like the other kids did, but I just couldn't.

The words didn't inspire me; they felt like rules and an attempt to control me. It wasn't like I was an anarchist and hated rules (I was a model student and avoided trouble whenever possible), but many of the Christian principles we were taught felt restrictive and cold—not at all what I envisioned a relationship with God could be. The more I tried to understand and conform to their definition of divinity, the more disconnected I felt. Following the rules of organized religion, even at such a young age, made me feel so mundanely *human*. Instead of feeling like a soulful, spiritual being made of stardust, connected to the Universe and an all-powerful being of love and light, I felt like an ant: powerless, aimless, and devoid of higher purpose.

Years later, after we'd stopped going to church, my younger sister Aya, who was nine, came home from school in tears. Her teacher had told her if a person wasn't baptized, they would go to Hell. Aya, filled with terror and conviction, told my mom she wanted to be baptized. I groaned—this meant we'd have to start going to church again, consistently, for an *entire year*! At first, I was annoyed by her decision, but when I looked into her face and realized how worried my precious sister was (about her eternal soul, no less!), my protective big sister instincts kicked in and I knew I had to do it for her. *Maybe it'll be different this time,* I thought. *Besides, it might be nice to have something to believe in.*

I was twelve and going through what would ultimately become one of the worst periods of my life. I was being bullied at school and learning how to live with newly-diagnosed anxiety. I hoped, *prayed*, that going to church would feel different this time. I desperately needed a place where I could feel safe, loved, and accepted, unconditionally.

On our first Sunday back, I showed up to church with an open mind and heart, but minutes after settling in to the hard wooden pew, Bible in hand, that same pit in my stomach returned. I was beyond disappointed and frustrated. I felt lost, like I was somehow hopelessly doomed to wander through life without any kind of belief system; like I'd never be able to connect to something that could ground me, but also nourish my soul. But I was there for Aya, so for weeks and months on end, I faked a smile, attended church, and endured the painful pit in my gut until finally, she got baptized.

Because I lived in Ottawa, the capital of Canada, I was surrounded by diversity and was regularly exposed to a kaleidoscope of cultures and beliefs. I had several friends who had very strong faith in their respective religions, and thought maybe I could find myself in one of their houses of worship. Through my friends, I learned about Hinduism, Islam, Sikhism, Judaism, and other denominations of Christianity, including Jehovah's Witnesses, Catholicism, and Unitarianism. I loved hearing about my friends' beliefs, and asked a ton of questions, hoping to discover something with which I could connect. But while my friends loved attending their churches, mosques, and temples, where they felt divine love and pure joy, nothing felt quite like my "divine destiny" or place of belonging.

For a while, disillusioned by religion and hopeless in my search, I adopted my dad's atheist beliefs. I decided to be content with the theory that we humans serve no greater purpose than to live, have a family, work hard, retire, and die. It seemed bleak, but nothing else really spoke to me.

The despair I felt as an atheist served me well as I transformed into an "emo" teenager. I was in a dark space: I listened to heavy metal and grunge rock music; wore all black; and basically spent every day feeling sorry for myself. I didn't know who I was or why I was here—my life was one giant pity party (I was basically a human Eeyore with too

28

much black eyeliner). I kept focusing on what I didn't want, what was going wrong for me, who didn't like me, and what I did poorly. For almost three years, I lived in a state of perpetual negativity.

Until one fateful Friday night.

I was seventeen and finally emerging from my "emo" phase (to the relief of my family). I had plans with friends to celebrate the start of another weekend, until my mom sat me and Aya down and told us we were having a family movie night.

"No way, I'm going out," I snarked, annoyed at my mother's audacity to suggest I should spend my precious Friday night with my family and not my friends

My mom insisted and we continued to argue, until one of my friends called and said our plans were cancelled. Damn it.

"Guess you're stuck with us after all," my mother said, smirking. She seemed so proud of herself, like she had somehow willed it to happen that way.

The movie she'd selected for us to watch was *The Secret*.[2] She'd heard about it through a friend at work and thought it would be inspiring for us to watch together as a family. To make matters worse, it was a documentary—not even a normal movie! It sounded dumb, and as I sat indignantly in front of the television, I criticized everything.

Soon I found myself leaning in, though. As various spiritual teachers, writers, scientists, and philosophers—from all walks of life—shared their wisdom, my demeanor changed.

Their words and ideas were like healing water upon desert sands; their truths washed over me and began to hydrate my malnourished soul. For so long I had silently wished for a deeper purpose and meaning to life and finally, for the first time, that craving was being satisfied.

Ninety-one minutes later, as the credits rolled, I was a changed person. I had opened up to a new way of not only thinking, but *being*, and somehow my teenage "woe is me" attitude melted away. The film made me realize that through my thoughts and words and actions, I'd been attracting all of the negativity I had claimed I didn't want. I thought about my boyfriend (at the time), and how all of my focus had been on the unfulfilling parts of our relationship, on everything he did to upset me, which had just created more animosity between us. I finally understood that I controlled my life: I had the power to choose and feel and do whatever I wanted, and those choices, feelings, and behaviors could either empower me, or destroy me.

This is where my deep spiritual work began but I knew I had a long journey ahead of me. I felt ready to devour as much information as I could about the Law of Attraction, which was the guiding principle of *The Secret*.

My research led me to the "Abraham-Hicks teachings."[3] Abraham is the representation of a collective of Divine energy, who is channeled through a woman named Esther Hicks. At first, it seemed odd and far-fetched, but as I listened to the teachings every day, I felt like I had found my spiritual truth. That awful pit in my stomach had been replaced with excitement and radiance.

The Law of Attraction is a Universal Law that is now supported even by quantum physics. Like the Law of Gravity, this law is always working for us, regardless of whether or not we realize or acknowledge it. We are either intentionally using the Law of Attraction to manifest a future we desire, or we are subconsciously and aimlessly co-creating our futures with it.

The Law of Attraction works with the energy and vibration of our thoughts and feelings. All matter consists of energy—the chair you're sitting on, the cup in your hand, this book you're reading, and even *you*. Everything in the Universe is and has energy, which can actually be measured with scientific instruments. Your emotional output has different energy frequencies, which attract similar experiences and circumstances. Put plainly: your thoughts and feelings determine what kind of life you have. The Universe functions like a mirror: if you stare into it with anger, that's what you will see; if you soften your gaze with a smile, that is what will reflect back.

Every time I listen to Abraham or re-watch (or read!) *The Secret*, the message is clear: the second we desire something, it is already created in energetic form. You don't have to see, smell, taste, or touch something to know it is real or possible to attain. The Universe will conspire to materialize whatever you think, feel, and desire—good or bad. Energy flows where attention goes. You must call what you want in, but mindfully; saying, "I don't want that!" still focuses on the thing you don't want, and the Universe responds to the vibration of your intention—positive *or* negative. Of course, every single positive thought doesn't result in a positive result, nor does every single negative thought trigger something awful to happen. It's about mastering consistent thoughts, cultivating repeated mindfulness, and trusting that things are unfolding as they are meant to.

The Secret and Abraham taught me to trust the power of the Universe. When you order food at a restaurant, you trust it will be brought to your table; you don't go check on the cook every two minutes to see if it's done yet. You placed your order, and you trust it will arrive (granted, it may not always be *exactly* what you ordered, but such is the way with the Universe!). I also learned that the Law of Attraction is about trusting the power within. If you had complete and total trust in your ability to create everything you desire, you could release the resistance and fear, and simply allow the desires to manifest, with Divine timing. The sooner you calibrate to happy, high feelings and vibrations, the easier it will be to bring in the things you want and love most!

If any of this feels new or scary, or you're suddenly terrified you've been attracting only terrible things to your life, relax. Take a deep breath. Most of us have been conditioned to take a linear, analytical approach to everything, so some of these concepts may feel overwhelming at first. Hopefully, what you'll learn through the course of this book is that all experiences, even the ones we label "bad," have the power to teach us a lesson, confirm what we don't want, or even activate a desire to create something completely different. This is not about toxic positivity or spiritual bypassing, which is what happens when people say things like, "Just be happy all the time and nothing bad will happen." That is not the point, nor is it realistic or helpful. Sometimes the greatest shifts come from the most difficult situations. The key is to learn how to identify the lesson, learn from it, and navigate out of the darkness by amplifying and affirming our deepest, brightest desires. What *The Secret* taught me that Friday night so many years ago was I had the power to change my thoughts, which could affect my feelings, which could alter my vibration, which could allow me to call in some of the most amazing people, experiences, and things of my life. And so can you.

As we walk along this journey together, bear in mind that the Law of Attraction can coexist with and complement whatever religion you follow or spiritual beliefs you have. When you have a high vibration that is positive and in alignment with what you want, you are more connected to the Divine, which is in alignment with God/the Universe. Whatever your belief, however you connect with the Divine, is beautiful and welcome here. The Law of Attraction, as well as the teachings in this book, are not meant to replace your existing beliefs, but work in tandem with them. You can utilize the Law of Attraction to connect deeper to the divinity within you, which will enable you to embody your full potential. Throughout the book I will use the terms Universe, God, Divine, Spirit, Guides, Goddess, and *Dea,* all of which, for me, connect me to my higher power. Please apply whatever words resonate most with you!

Chapter 3

The Fall of the Feminine

For years as a pre-teen, I would awaken from nightmares of fire. I didn't know why I was having these terrifying dreams, nor where my overwhelming fear of fire came from. Finally one day, after I'd had yet another disruptive night of sleep, my mom resolutely said, "I think you were a witch in a past life, and you were burned at the stake." At first I thought she was nuts; I was barely in the beginning stages of my spiritual journey, and wasn't quite ready to accept that I'd had a past life, let alone spent it as a persecuted witch.

I didn't know anything about witches (*true* witches, not the Halloween variety) other than what I'd seen depicted in movies and TV shows, so I decided to do some research. I learned that the women we've labeled as witches in past centuries were actually midwives, herbal medicine doctors, and energy healers. These were women who existed decades, *centuries*, before any kind of women's equality movement or modern feminism existed. They understood their Divine power, feminine intuition, and connection with nature and the Universe. Today we accept these sorts of women as doulas, new age spiritual leaders, mediums, acupuncturists, and Reiki healers, but even in our modern society, they can still be outcasts, misunderstood, and labeled as "eccentric."

The witches of the past were blamed for all sorts of crises in the world. When the Plague spread in the 1300s, killing thirty percent of Europe's population, the Catholic Church pointed the finger at the "devil-worshipping witches."[4] Over the next three hundred years, witch hunts spread throughout Europe, and an estimated 80,000 women were burned alive or hung for "doing the devil's work." In the name of God, tens of thousands of innocent women, who probably would have done immense good in their communities, were brutally murdered.[5]

This is one of the most notable examples of the "human masculine" snuffing out the Divine Feminine. The human masculine is very logical and systematic, and is responsible for having shaped and molded most religions, governmental systems, and societal constructs we participate in today. Balanced spirituality recognizes the Divine Masculine and Divine Feminine, but humankind has become increasingly unbalanced over time, which has led to rigid, patriarchal dogma and the human masculine need for power over Divine purpose.

The best example of this comes from nearly two thousand years ago. In 313 AD, Emperor Constantine (Rome's first Christian emperor) issued the Edict of Milan, granting Christianity legal status within the Roman Empire (this was a major step because for years, Christians had been considered enemies to the empire because they would not worship the Roman gods). Then, twenty-two years later, Constantine called together the Council of Nicaea, with the purpose of creating an orthodox religion. It was at this point that Christianity shifted from a mystical, spiritual movement to a more rigid, organized religion. The new Christianity, under Constantine's rule, became a political tool for control. The final elimination of mysticism within Christian spirituality came in 380 AD, when Emperor Theodosius enacted the Edict of Thessalonica, which made Christianity the official religion of the Roman Empire. All other sects outside of the newly established Christian orthodoxy were deemed heresy, and the followers of the more mystical movements were persecuted. [6]

I've come to realize that this patriarchal, human masculine version of Christianity is why I had difficulty connecting to church as a young girl: the *Dea* within me felt suffocated. My soul yearned to awaken, to connect and communicate with the Divine Feminine, and to find a mystic balance within myself.

Through the work and research I have done, I've been astonished to discover that nearly every ancient culture and religion have included masculine and feminine polarity in some form. Many, in fact, worshipped a plethora of gods and goddesses, who represented various aspects of both human life and divinity.

Yogic traditions have been around for thousands of years, with a vast depth of different practices—many of which honor both the Divine Feminine and Divine Masculine. Yoga is intended to balance one's yin and yang energy: the left and right side of the body. The word "Yoga" means union: the joining of our physical being with the Divine.[7] While most westerners associate Yoga with a series of stretches and poses (*asanas*) meant to cultivate good physical health and overall well-being, Yoga as a spiritual practice is so much more: it's about freeing the soul from one's body and mind; elevating one's Divine self. Tantra is a yogic devotional practice that specifically celebrates Divine Feminine power (it's not just about sex, as it has been so wildly misunderstood and misrepresented in western culture).[8]

In Hindu culture, there is also a balance of power between the Divine Masculine and Divine Feminine. The god Shiva represents the Divine Masculine. He is the destroyer, but also represents rebirth and renewal. The goddess Shakti encompasses all of the Divine Feminine. She is a universal, Divine Feminine energy force, responsible for creation, destroying evil, and fostering balance. She is the mother goddess, the true archetype of Divine Feminine power. Shakti can take form as other goddesses, including Parvati, Durga, and Kali. She is a *mahadevi,* which means "great goddess" in Sanskrit; basically, Shakti is the representation of all goddesses in one, and there are countless temples devoted to her where Hindus worship and celebrate the Divine Feminine. Yet neither Shiva nor Shakti is more powerful than the other; they need each other. What we can learn from Hinduism is that we all possess masculine *and* feminine energies, and we benefit most when we embrace and balance both sides.[9]

The ancient Chinese worshipped and celebrated over 200 gods and goddesses, including the goddess Guanyin. I first learned about Guanyin when I visited the Nelson Atkins Art Museum in Kansas City, Missouri. As I entered the ancient China exhibit, I stumbled into a room where I saw a stunning statue. I could barely breathe; she was so powerful and beautiful. I stood there for several minutes, staring at her, feeling mesmerized by her energy. Guanyin was one of many goddesses in ancient China featured in that exhibit, but for some reason I felt deeply, cosmically connected to her. She is the *bodhisattva* (a person who is on an enlightened path, usually on their way to becoming a Buddha) of compassion; the Goddess of Mercy. Another Buddhist goddess is Tara, who rises from the mud on a beautiful blossoming lotus flower. She appears in many Buddhist cultures, most often in Tibet, Nepal, and Mongolia.

In Tibet, Tara is believed to incarnate within every woman devoted to their spiritual journey—a beautiful example of discovering the goddess within![10]

Wicca, a modern pagan religious movement, explores the magic of universal laws (primarily through prayers and intention ceremonies) and honors the gods and goddesses who govern the earth and sky. Wiccans believe in the balance of masculine and feminine energies, and how that balance helps our planet thrive. Wicca's core values are to respect the earth and all beings on it, and to "do no harm."[11]

Numerous religions and cultures have honored the Divine Feminine throughout the course of history, but unfortunately, fear has tried to keep the Divine Feminine from thriving. The Divine Feminine, which wants to expand, learn, and flow, threatens organizations, religions, and world leaders who are resistant to change. The patriarchy, driven by the human masculine need for power and control, fears the Divine Feminine's truth and light. For centuries, women have been ridiculed, tortured, exiled, rejected, attacked, and even murdered for having the courage to express their Divine Feminine power. Like the fire in my dreams, the patriarchy has tried to keep us up at night, afraid of tapping into our potential and discovering who we might truly be: powerful and divine vessels of the Universe.

This fear of feminine power has led to an imbalance of Divine energy, which in turn has caused severe division, hatred and bigotry, and war. My heart breaks thinking about how much good has been eradicated by greed and violence. The warped lens of the human masculine has convinced us that our differences divide us, the "other" is to be feared, and money and power are more important than connection and empathy. Our planet, Mother Earth, the *ultimate* Divine

Feminine power, is in pain, too. We are in the midst of a global climate crisis as sacred land gets over-developed, natural habitats are replaced by steel and concrete, and animal species continue to be endangered and eradicated. There is ongoing drilling for and refining of fossil fuels, which not only violates the earth, but also creates alarming amounts of waste in the process. The oceans are littered with floating garbage that chokes seabirds and suffocates underwater wildlife. Our cities are smothered in smog, the fast fashion industry has resulted in overconsumption and underpaid labor, and our food is the least nourishing it has ever been due to genetic modifications and chemical pesticides.

For too long, women have been treated as the weaker sex. We've been objectified, categorized, and marginalized. We have been paid less for doing the same (if not superior) work, and yet our buying power has been exploited by male-owned corporations who charge premiums for the things we buy (namely personal hygiene items like menstrual products, haircuts, dry-cleaning services, and razors—this has been dubbed the "pink tax" and it's appalling. Statistics have found that women pay more than men for the same products or services 42% of the time.[12]

The root of spirituality and the Divine Feminine is Love—for oneself and others. Through learning more about our Divine Feminine power, and other cultures and religions that embrace it, we can learn to love and appreciate ourselves, flaws and all, and have more patience and understanding for those who appear different than us.* We need to model ourselves and learn from indigenous cultures that have been tending to and honoring Mother Earth for countless generations. Businesses and corporations need to switch focus from stockholders and profits to the planet and people.

And our governments need to embrace renewable energies and environmentally-friendly technologies. This is the only path to eradicating the planet's collective pain and achieving global harmony.

We have work to do. The world needs us to get back in touch with our inner goddesses, with our Divine Feminine, so we can shine our light, spread goodness and truth, and open up to one another (and we must be mindful of how we can help our sisters in countries where they are not as free to express their Divine Feminine power). As our collective feminine energy grows and spreads, there will be an influx of new ideas, female-owned businesses and non-profit organizations, and women in positions of political and social spheres of influence.

You have a unique message and mission, and the world is waiting for you to restore balance with your Divine Feminine energy. Maybe you are afraid to let your light shine because of something that happened in your past (perhaps your past *life*!), but I assure you, this is a safe space and we are entering a new age where you can be the powerful goddess you are. Your story can and will be different now, so long as you are ready for growth and change, remain open, and serve on behalf of the greater good. We are in this together, and I believe in you, *Dea*.

*FOOTNOTE Though this book contains a message of Love, it would be remiss of me not to mention that there is a time and place for discernment. Causing trauma, abusing power, or taking advantage of others is never okay. Divine balance does not always mean "peace and love," though of course I pray for a golden age when peace and love are all we know. True balance requires vocal, passionate dissent when harm is being done. Your inner goddess will help steer you towards justice, truth, and equality!

Chapter 4

Masculine and Feminine

As you read in the previous chapter, a balance between masculine and feminine energies is essential to being at peace with oneself and bringing serenity to the planet. Let's explore the differences between these energies, and how they manifest in our daily lives. *Please note: The Divine Feminine and Masculine transcend gender and sexual orientation. The terms feminine and masculine are part of everyday human language, and do not truly reflect your cosmic energy or connection to Divine power. Feel free to use other labels if that feels more authentic for you.*

Feminine energy is more right brain: it lends itself to intuition and artistic thinking, with a focus on creativity, compassion, and understanding. Like the moon, it is reflective and illuminates dark spaces. The Divine Feminine is loving, nurturing, confident, sensual, knowing, and powerful. She sets boundaries and doesn't permit people to walk all over her. She holds people accountable to their greater selves, which can involve difficult conversations or "tough love." The Divine Feminine does not judge, but listens and sees the good in all. She is a creator—she can literally *and* metaphorically form and birth new life. She is a healer and possesses a sincere reverence and tremendous love for all living creatures: the earth, her fellow humans, plants, animals, and of course, herself. Anyone can access their Divine Feminine side to be more creative, intuitive, empathic, and caring, or to express truth and emotions more easily.

Masculine energy is more left brain and leads to more linear thoughts and ideas, thriving on logic, science, and mathematics or equations. Like the sun, it thrives on power and strength. The Divine Masculine is protective, logical, and action-oriented. He is strong, loyal, and does the right thing. He is a leader, creates plans, and is self-motivated, as well as self-disciplined. Tapping into this aspect of your inner being can encourage you to take more confident action. The Divine Masculine can also help you feel more secure and safe.

One energy is not more important than the other; we need both, equally, though we will rarely experience both with the same intensity, at the same time (stay tuned for chapter 10, in which we will discuss how to tap into different energies depending on the time of our cycle). We all have masculine and feminine energies within us, and it is our Divine duty to balance and honor them.

Most women have been taught to silence their Divine powers, both Masculine and Feminine, and live submissively to men. We've been told our feminine qualities make us weak, and that being emotional and intuitive makes us less powerful. As a result, your goddess may have been lulled to sleep, lying dormant within you as you've attempted to navigate the restrictions of the human masculine world. And in spite of being favored by the patriarchy, most men are imbalanced as well, denying, or ignorant to, the full potential of their Divine power.

Regardless of gender, we all have work to do on healing our relationships with our Divine energies: Feminine, Masculine, or both. Many of us have been clinging to misconceptions about feminine and masculine traits: the feminine is overly emotional, weak, and needy or desperate for external love/fulfillment; the masculine is hurtful, ravenous for sex with no emotional attachment, and will abandon you. None of these perceptions are Divine; rather, they are foibles of being human and are sabotaging our Divine power. We miss out on so much of ourselves when we cut off access to our Divine Feminine or Masculine. Past trauma or abuse, particularly toxic romantic relationships, may have detached you from your Divine power but now is the time to release all of the stigma, pain, and judgement. The biggest gift you can give yourself, and your inner goddess, is to forgive and heal.

I recently had the opportunity to participate in a very healing women's circle. It happened to fall on the night of *Mahashivaratri*, a Hindu festival that honors the marriage of the god Shiva and the goddess Parvati. This celebration represents the unity of the Divine Masculine and Feminine. During the ceremony, we went around the room and shared our intentions for what we wanted to forgive and release.

I was blown away by how similar nearly every woman's wounds were. My fellow goddesses disclosed negative experiences with being deceived, abandoned, and abused. There was so much pain in that room that by the end we were emotional and raw, filled with grief and empathy for one another. A sisterhood—based on safety, love, and healing comfort—had been established, which enabled us to dig deeper.

The leader of the event began the healing work by explaining that pain actually has nothing to do with the Divine; pain is a human emotion inflicted by human behavior. Before we could move towards working with our Divine Feminine and Masculine energies, we needed to forgive the people who had hurt us.

I anticipated hearing that many of the women were holding on to heartache associated with men, which was keeping them from connecting with or appreciating their Divine Masculine power. What I didn't expect was how many women were debilitated by deep-seated resentment towards *other women*. I heard dramatic stories about female friendships riddled with back-stabbing, guilt trips, manipulation, and betrayal—all of which had led to a mistrust of women and an inability to connect with their Divine Feminine. These women had spent years avoiding any kind of sisterhood, relying solely on relationships, both platonic and romantic (and often toxic) with men.

I became conscious of two very powerful things that evening. The first was, women need to be able to build positive, trusting, nurturing, loving relationships with other women, in safe spaces away from human masculine influence. The other realization was too many of us prevent ourselves from aligning with our Divine power because we are avoiding the hard work of forgiving those who have hurt us (which will, in turn, allow us to heal).

Forgive

"It's one of the greatest gifts you can give yourself, to forgive. Forgive everybody." - Maya Angelou (Poet)

I've experienced the freeing feeling of forgiveness many times, but I remember one particular occasion vividly. I was finishing a yoga class. The room's lighting was dimmed, and I was lying in *Savasana* (also known as "Corpse Pose," where you lie on your back with your arms resting on the floor at your sides), with a relaxed mind and an open heart. The teacher slowly walked around the room and said, "Think of the word 'forgiveness.' See what comes up for you." Caught completely unaware, I started to cry.

46

I was holding onto pain and rejection caused by an uncomfortable "on again, off again" situation with a male friend. I was so unhappy, stuck in a cycle of victimhood and blame. For months, I'd been carrying the prideful weight of: "He did this to me. He doesn't deserve my forgiveness. I am going to hold on to this anger and pain." I was spending all of my precious energy trying to punish him, but I was actually just making myself feel terrible.

As I lied on my yoga mat, processing the word "forgiveness" over and over again, I felt the inner torment dissolve; my malice towards my friend washed away with every tear (and there were *many* tears). All of the tortured emotions released because I finally chose to feel love for my friend, and forgive him—and myself—for the situation we were in.

Moving forward from the class, I found myself feeling more harmony and less discord in my life. I created new, solid friendships because I was no longer wrapped up in a broken one. It was a simple, but profound shift. I had chosen to forgive the human masculine in my life, which opened me up to receive more of the Divine. I now had the confidence of knowing I was enough as I was, regardless of anyone else's opinions of or desire for me.

Forgiveness frees us to focus on the things and people that make us feel good. Forgiving someone does not mean what they did was okay, but releases you from the burden of needing to hold them accountable for your pain. Choosing not to forgive prevents you from being able to heal.

Heal

"You hold the keys to your own healing." - Martha Beck (Author)

Forgiveness itself can be quite healing, but usually there is more work to be done. It's nearly impossible to heal and thrive when most of your time is spent just trying to survive. For millennia, humanity's primary focus was on procuring food, finding water, and securing shelter—basic human needs. However, as we have industrialized and achieved huge advancements in technology, we've gotten very comfortable. This comfort has led us to become sedentary—in our bodies, minds, and souls. A shockingly high percentage of the world's population suffers from depression and anxiety (conditions from which I personally have had to heal), stress, addiction, and numerous other disorders, in spite of the fact that we have virtually every creature comfort at our disposal. Our survival has transitioned from basic physiological needs to mental, emotional, and spiritual ones.

Unfortunately, surviving is difficult when we are out of alignment with the Divine. Too many of us spend our days trapped in a monotonous cycle of unfulfillment: wake up and commute to a job; spend the day confined to a cubicle, executing a series of mundane tasks to avoid disapproval from a superior; commute home, where we numb ourselves (through alcohol, drugs, television, and countless other vices); and go to bed, depleted, drained, and disillusioned. This cycle is caused by the affliction of the human masculine (need for money, power, perceived strength, control), and could be healed or reinvigorated with a renewed focus on the Divine Masculine (desire to serve, grow, expand, motivate, innovate, and empower).

Women, while also trapped in this human masculine cycle, have additionally been forced to disconnect from their intuitive, creative natures (Divine Feminine) and as a result, have also found themselves numbing the stressors of life with unhealthy habits (such as drugs, alcohol, smoking, and eating disorders). Women are not only expected to be high achievers (appealing to the human masculine), but also caretakers who serve others (typically at great cost to their own wellbeing).

Humanity is sick, more worried about the material than the spiritual; on doing and getting and having more than on becoming. We're more focused on winning, as opposed to growing into the greatest, most ascended versions of ourselves.

Recently I listened to an audio recording of someone receiving a "channeling" from Gautama Buddha. The message they received mentioned that the cause of the devastating amount of depression and anxiety these days is a result of our resistance to the healing light trying to come into our world. Abraham-Hicks says, "There is only a stream of well-being that flows. You can allow it or resist it, but it flows just the same." We have a choice every moment of every day to resist the light and stay in the darkness, or allow the well-being, love, divinity, and wholeness innately within us to flow. Taking time to heal will allow your Divine source to flow more easily and abundantly. Your light is already within you; it wants to shine brightly but it needs you to stop blotting it out with the darkness of blame, victimhood, resentment, and fear.

Grow

"And the day came when the risk to remain tight in a bud was more painful than the risk it took to blossom." - Anais Nin (Writer)

Once we forgive and heal, we are more equipped to grow (though certainly tremendous growth also occurs during those first two stages). Our souls, brains, and bodies crave growth, but sadly we have been conditioned (by the human masculine) to resist change because it requires leaving our comfort zones. Comfort zones are "safe" and mean we get to live in the familiarity of the status quo without having to exert too much energy, risk failure, or possibly look wrong or foolish. They can look like steady jobs, stale relationships, or friendships that rely on the "good ol' days" or partying to stay afloat. Comfort zones allow us to be part of the herd, protected from jeers or criticism. When we stray from the monochromatic crowd in search of change and growth, we risk having our loved ones reject us; so we stay, and more often than not, we wither away from the monotony.

We'll talk more about growth in later chapters, but I want to emphasize now how important having a growth mindset is. The more you venture beyond the borders of your comfort zone, the more acclimated you become to being uncomfortable (they're called "*growing* pains" for a reason!). We're never truly "comfortable" inside the cage of our comfort zone, but because it's familiar territory, we stay. We remain confined to the cage, until it finally becomes unbearable; this metaphorical claustrophobia acts as a catalyst for breaking out of the cage.

I encourage you to embrace the fact that the work will never end, but evolve and deepen. The more you honor and cultivate the Divine Masculine and Feminine, the closer you'll be to awakening your inner goddess.

SOUL WORK

Grab your special notebook or journal and write down everything you love about yourself. See if you can categorize these qualities as either Divine Masculine or Divine Feminine. Do you feel balanced? Is one more dominant? Are there qualities that are typically Divine Masculine or Feminine you wish you could see in yourself? Do you associate more negative feelings with one side or the other?

Take some time to forgive these qualities you dislike about yourself (or perhaps in other people). If it's helpful, have an imaginary conversation with or write a letter to yourself (or a person who has caused you pain). Say or write down *everything*. Be completely honest and vulnerable in your expression. At the end, declare that you are releasing the pain and sending love and light to yourself/the person who harmed you. You don't have to mail the letter (unless you want to!); remember that ultimately forgiveness is about *you*, not them. You can burn or shred it, crumple it up, or save it—whatever feels right and most beneficial to you.

Share your experience online with #IdeaSoulWork.

Chapter 5

Creating Space

Your life is like a precious keepsake box: inside, there is only so much space; when the box is full, you have to search through the box to find something you no longer need, in order to add something new. Living the life of your dreams will require you to give up your old life and to do so, you must create space.

When you cling to old mindsets and feelings about money, you cannot expect to attract abundance. When you want to call in love and passion, you cannot be fixated on failed relationships or heartache. When you hate and speak negative words about yourself, how can you ever expect your inner goddess to appear? Like with an overcrowded closet or overflowing dresser drawers, there is no room for the new until we bless and release (and in some literal cases, *throw out*) the old. Intention is the seed of every manifestation: what do you want, and have you created space for it?

The Law of Attraction states that what you focus on—positive or negative—grows. Vibrationally, you cannot be focused on the solution and the problem at the same time; they're not on the same wavelengths. Focusing on what makes you feel good (solutions) more than on what feels bad (the problems) can be challenging if you haven't cleared away enough of the stuff that is no longer serving you. This is not about ignoring problems, or *never* thinking negative thoughts, but learning how to channel your energy towards constructive choices and releasing worry, control, and other toxic emotions more quickly so as not to make your problems bigger than they actually are. Creating space results in clarity, which facilitates stronger manifestation through the Law of Attraction.

Before we begin to create space, I want you to activate your imagination and visualize what you'd like to create space *for*.

You are a beautiful, vibrant goddess living your most abundant, fabulous life. What does your home look like? Your room, bathroom, and closet? With whom do you share your life? What foods do you eat? What do your clothes look like? What do *you* look like? How do you stand? What do you say to yourself in the mirror? How do you spend your time?

Now take a moment to consider how your answers above differ from your current state. Can you identify places in your present circumstances where you could clear space for the big dreams above? How can you make that stunning goddess feel cherished, happy, safe, and proud? Are you ready to make space for the new life you are co-creating with your *Dea*?

It's time to take out the garbage—in your home, body, mind, and soul.

Creating space in your home first may seem superficial, but I assure you, it's a great way to ease into this process. Seeing visible, physical space open up in your environment will empower and motivate you to tackle other areas of your life. Go through every room, closet, cupboard, and drawer— even your car! Organize your workspace by going through stacks of paper or mail that have accumulated. File what needs to be kept and toss or recycle the rest. Throw out what is broken, worn out, and/or covered in dust (and recycle whenever possible!). Donate clothes, shoes, jewelry, dishes, and furniture you don't like, wear, use, or need anymore. Pass these items along to friends, local shelters, or second-hand/consignment stores. Use your favorite search engine to figure out how to recycle or donate more unique items like bras, electronics, old paint, etc. You can even do this with your digital spaces: organize the files on your computer's desktop; delete/file emails from your inbox; unfollow social media accounts that don't inspire you; and delete outdated text/messenger threads. Creating space in your home and work environments will reflect in your energy and allow you to focus on other important things.

Your body is a miraculous vessel and your most important "home," so it only makes sense to clean it out and create space for better things from time to time. Reset your health by focusing on feeding your body whole, organic foods from the earth—plant-based, as much as possible. Stop, or at least scale back on, eating highly processed foods, sugar, dairy, and gluten, and try to reduce your consumption of caffeine and alcohol. Try this for one week and see how you feel! This is about progress, not perfection, and it's never about shame. Love your body enough to treat it like a temple. Nourish your body with food that will not only help you survive, but *thrive*.

Show gratitude for whatever food you choose to consume. Enjoy every bite and be thankful for the plants, animals, and people who contributed to you having the opportunity to eat. Changing your relationship with food will create space for you to have a much more positive relationship with your body.

In addition to food, what else are you consuming and absorbing on a daily basis? Are your personal care products and supplements helping you create an internal environment of optimal health? Are you having uplifting conversations, or engaging in gossip and complaining? What sorts of TV shows, movies, music, etc., are you watching and listening to? Are you intentional about the energy you allow into your life? Be conscious about avoiding toxins in all forms: food, products, the environment, and even other people. Your body is affected by all of it.

Spend time with your body the same way you would with a romantic partner. Treat it to a good meal, take a bath, indulge in a massage. Spend time thanking every bit of your body, from your head to your toes, for what it does for you. And get moving! Moving your body every day will also help create space. By releasing pent up energy, you avoid stagnancy and make room for a more fit and flexible physique (whatever that looks like for *you*).

Learning how to appreciate your body and create space for health and vitality is no easy feat for many of us who have grown up in a society that constantly shames us (especially women) for looking certain ways. How can we expect our dream bodies to appear if we constantly send them messages of disapproval, hatred, and judgement? Our words affect every cell of our being; if we want our bodies to change, we have to change what we feed them, how we move them, and most importantly—what we say to and think about them!

"And I said to my body softly, 'I want to be your friend.'
It took a long breath and replied, 'I've been waiting my
whole life for this.'" - Nayyirah Waheed (Poet)

Be aware of the words you say and thoughts you think on a daily basis. What messages do you have on repeat? Abraham-Hicks teaches that a belief is a thought you keep thinking; therefore, you can change your beliefs by changing your consistent thoughts. It takes work and practice, but rewiring your brain with new thoughts will change your life.

Did you know you are made up of about sixty percent water? Doctor Masaru Emoto was a Japanese scientist who completely changed the way we understand the power of intention and human consciousness. In order to examine the power of our thoughts and words, Emoto would flash freeze water molecules and expose them to positive (or "pleasant") versus negative (or "unpleasant") words, phrases, thoughts, feelings, music, and sounds. What he discovered was incredible: the structure of the water molecules changed based on whether they were subjected to something positive or negative. The positive impact transformed the water into clear, beautiful, symmetrical masterpieces that resembled snowflakes. When the water reacted to negative feedback, it looked dark, dirty, and deformed.[13] If over half of your body composition is water, imagine what your insides look like depending on what you say, think, or feel!

The popular furniture store IKEA organized a similar experiment as part of an anti-bullying campaign. They wanted to illustrate how important it was to spread kindness and positivity. IKEA donated two plants to a school. Each one was placed in a clear, protective case with a speaker, so the students could hear what was being played. One speaker played uplifting affirmations for its plant (like a friend), while the other played words of discouragement (like a bully). By the end of the experiment, the friendly plant stood tall, and was vibrantly green, but the bullied plant had wilted.[14] I was so moved when I read about this because I remembered being bullied and how much it had impacted my self-esteem. When I am surrounded by life-affirming friends, family, and colleagues, I too stand tall and proud. It made me so happy to know those students were learning that lesson early in life; and now I want YOU to benefit from it, too!

You can actually do your own very simple test to illustrate this phenomenon. Put dry, uncooked rice in two jars and then fill them with water (make sure there are equal amounts of rice and water in each jar). On one jar, write "LOVE" and on the other, write "HATE." Every day, send affirming, loving words, thoughts, and feelings to the LOVE jar, and mean, angry ones to the HATE jar. When I did this for thirty days, the "love" rice had fermented without any mold—it was white and plump. The "hate" rice, however, had turned to black, moldy mush. It was amazing! If you wind up doing this experiment, please share your results online with #IdeaSoulWork.

What these experiments so clearly and simply illustrate is that WORDS AND THOUGHTS HAVE POWER. Imagine saying the mean, negative things we say to ourselves to a sweet innocent baby. We would never! Imagine saying them to your very best friend. We wouldn't dream of it! Now imagine saying them to a Divine goddess. We would be horrified! My Sister, you are all three: you are a perfect miracle of life with an inner child who hears everything you say; you are your best friend, and the person with whom you spend the most time; and you, dear goddess, are a Divine being and the power of the Universe is within you. When you talk to yourself, imagine you are the baby, your best friend, a goddess, and *speak life* into and around yourself. Stop tearing yourself down with negative words and thoughts—many of which are the result of societal, human masculine conditioning.

"Rewiring" our thoughts takes time, patience, and practice. Incorporate positive affirmations into your day, *every* day, and say them with energy and passion. Whenever possible, make eye contact with yourself in a mirror and say, "I love you." I remember the first time I finally did this—it was an illuminating experience.

It was a Wednesday, like every other Wednesday. I crawled out of bed, went into the bathroom, and grabbed my toothbrush. As I was going through the motions of my mundane morning routine, glancing at my messy hair, mismatched pajamas, and dreary eyes, a wave of energy washed over me. I suddenly had an epiphany: *Every time I look in the mirror, I only look at my reflection.* I'd only ever focused on the things I viewed as "wrong" or in need of "fixing," like my thighs, or stomach, or acne. I was always judging the girl in the mirror, instead of looking into the eyes of the goddess before me.

I set my toothbrush down and leaned in. I stared intensely into my own eyes, and really looked *into* myself—saw the *real* me. I was overcome with love for the woman before me. I saw her wounds *and* her achievements, her potential and passion, her vibrancy and spirit. I put my hands on opposite shoulders, closed my eyes, and embraced myself. I hugged the goddess within. I apologized to Her for all of the self-doubt, criticism, and judgement. And then I looked back into my eyes and said, "I love you so much." Tears streamed down my face and I smiled, knowing I had finally started to make peace with myself.

We all want to be seen, heard, and loved for who we are by others, yet we rarely offer such kindness to ourselves (or when we do, it is usually conditional). "I love myself, *but...*" or "I'll like my body *when...*" or "I'd be happy *if...*" The only way we can begin to be whole, and expect others to love and respect us in our truest, most authentic forms, is by learning to love and respect ourselves unconditionally. Listen to and honor your needs, as opposed to waiting for others to fulfill them. Find moments to be still with yourself, and listen to what your mind and heart (and *Dea!*) are telling you.

SOUL WORK

Create a morning ritual during which you sit with yourself (and your *Dea*) and share what you will be releasing and calling in that day.

As you spend time visualizing the abundance you wish to attract to your life, consider making a vision board. Having a creative outlet for your vision is not only fun, but also extremely effective for helping you stay committed to your goals. Literally construct the scenes of your dream life and in turn, through looking at them every day, you are far more likely to manifest them. This doesn't have to be fancy—grab a piece of cardboard or even a plain piece of paper, and make a collage from magazine clippings or images you print from online. Make sure that the images inspire you and make you feel excited.

When I made my first vision board, I added a spectacular photo of Atlantis Paradise Island. Four months later, my company announced that the upcoming incentive trip was going to be held at that very resort! And one year after I made my board, I was on the trip, living out my vision in the Bahamas. I worked very hard, but setting the intention and affirming my goal everyday created the magic that drove me to achieve my big dream.

In addition to your vision board, I highly recommend keeping a notebook or journal (maybe the one you're using for your Soul Work!) that can become your "vision book." This will allow you to carry your big dreams and goals everywhere with you (like a written version of your vision board), and add to them as new ideas and wishes come to mind. I also like to use mine to recount dreams I've had, create new affirmations, etc. Occasionally I'll include a photo if it's something from my vision board I want to see while I'm traveling or working outside of my home. Before bed every night, make a ritual of going through your vision book. Absorb every word and picture, and read each affirmation (aloud, if you can). This way, you fall asleep visualizing the new you and the fabulous life you want to manifest.

Now go back and revisit the list of Divine Masculine and Feminine qualities you wrote down. Which ones would you like to experience more often, or in greater quantity? Turn these into "I AM" affirmations you can recite every day (I highly recommend writing them on your mirror or on sticky notes you put around the house).

If this all feels new and you can't think of any yet, try these!

I AM powerful beyond measure!
I AM healthy and energetic!

I AM self-motivated!
I AM intuitive and trust my inner guidance!
I AM confident in my own skin!
I AM worthy of an amazing life!
I AM sharing my light with the world!
I AM successful and attract abundance!
I AM a GODDESS!

Share your experience online with #IdeaSoulWork.

Chapter 6

Ancestral Patterns

There is a healing technique called Access Consciousness[15] (also known as Access Bars) that is designed to help you release limiting thoughts and beliefs. I won't go into too many details of what the treatment entails (though I highly recommend you look it up!), but what I've found in researching it is that nearly all of the restricting ideas and attitudes we carry with us rarely belong to us. We walk through life stressed and drained, usually because we're trying to solve problems for other people (our boss, spouse, kids, parents, colleagues, friends, neighbors, etc.) or we're carrying the weight of things over which we have little to no control (politics, the news, etc.). You may even randomly absorb problematic energy from complete strangers!

Feeling obligated to assist other people does not come from a true desire to help or be in service. I hadn't realized I'd spent nearly two decades trapped in this unhealthy pattern until after I started spending time with my boyfriend Dylan's family. On one visit to his family's home in Kansas, we spent a day driving around with his mom Christy, whom I really admired and respected. I was complaining about all of the things I "had" to do for other people and how they were stressing me out, costing me money, and preventing me from spending time building my health and wellness business. When I finally ran out of steam, Christy gently said, "Sweetie, why are you doing all of this? Do you actually want to do these things?" I was dumbfounded. It had genuinely never occurred to me I was allowed to say no to other people's requests.

What I learned that day, and through observing Christy (who is very successful), was if you say yes to everything that is asked of you, or agree to attend every event to which you are invited, you will never have time for the things that matter to you (remember, we must *create space* for the things we want!). Christy inspired me not to be afraid to say no to things that do not bring me joy, positively impact my business, help my family, or create abundance. The choice was mine: burn out for others or live for myself. I'd always been afraid of looking selfish or missing out or being disliked by other people but once I gave myself permission not to worry about those things, I became more open to new and exciting opportunities.

Access Consciousness teaches you to ask yourself, "Does this [feeling, idea, belief, thought] belong to me?" If the answer is no, then you respond by saying, "Return to sender with love and consciousness." Release the guilt of saying no to things that do not serve you or your *Dea's* higher purpose.

Though you can free up a great deal of mental and emotional bandwidth by saying no to solving other people's problems, there will always be deeply rooted patterns and ideas within that demand attention—many of which we inherit from our ancestors.

Energy, belief systems, behaviors, and even trauma can be passed down from your parents, your grandparents, and so on. When negative thoughts are embedded at a cellular level, it can feel extremely difficult, nearly impossible, to break free and create space for new, more positive ways of thinking. The following are generalizations, but strong examples of what some of these damaging ancestral patterns can look like.

For instance, men can be very hard on each other. They call each other names and jab one another's egos. Men typically hide their emotions and are not comfortable having open heart conversations with other men. These patterns have usually been passed down from grandfather to father to son, pressured by the human masculine need not to appear weak or feminine. Men stay in their comfort zones and do what is "expected" of them: work hard, provide, and remain impervious to feelings. They will often numb this ancestral pain by adopting harmful behaviors such as drinking, drugging, gambling, engaging in emotionally detached, high-risk sexual behavior, or playing excessive amounts of violent video games. To help the men in our lives heal from this pain and allow in more of the Divine Feminine, we must create safe spaces for them to express their emotions, be vulnerable, and feel heard.

Women may experience similar ancestral patterns, of course, but usually our inherited pain looks more like people pleasing, feeling inferior to men, unworthiness, competition with other women, and perfectionism (in our relationships, bodies, jobs etc.). These patterns, which result from an oppressive patriarchy designed to keep us from recognizing our Divine power and rising up, have often been passed down from grandmother to mother to daughter.

Perfectionism is a particularly nasty trait we women inherit (if not from our ancestors, then certainly from society). We are expected to look "conventionally beautiful," which typically means thin—but not *too* thin, or *too* muscular, or *too* sexy—and resembling some westernized Euro-centric colonial "ideal." We're expected to behave modestly, be delicate and feminine, please our partners, tend to our children, maintain our households, and succeed in our careers. We're expected to execute all of this, at the same time, perfectly, without resentment or complaint. No wonder our goddesses are asleep—they're exhausted! And all too often, when a woman starts to connect with her Divine self, she winds up abandoning her dreams because she is made to feel guilty or ashamed for prioritizing herself.

These types of ancestral patterns have especially manifested in more recent generations, as heteronormative gender roles wane and the economy changes. Over the past seventy years or so, more and more women have entered the workforce. This has been empowering for women, but it has also bred new forms of ancestral guilt and shame because they have ventured beyond the comfort zones of their mothers and grandmothers. I've noticed this in my own family, in fact.

As a young woman, my mom dreamed of becoming an actress, but her family told her she should "just get a good secretarial job." While of course there is nothing wrong with being a secretary, these words shattered my mom's dreams and self-esteem. When I first announced I was going to be an entrepreneur (as opposed to getting a traditional "nine-to-five" office job), some of my adult family members said things like, "Can't you just get a real job?" and "But you're so young, no one will listen to you." They'd say, "You actually think you're going to make it?" and "That sort of thing never works." At the time, their words hurt me and made me feel unworthy. This held me back in my business and life for years, until I realized they weren't saying those things to be malicious. I eventually recognized their words stemmed from fear—a place of ingrained doubt and pain, passed down to them through a system intent on keeping them inside their comfort zones.

Fear can be useful; it is implanted within us to help us remain alive and protect us from danger. Fear typically can be narrowed down to three types: fear for our bodily safety; fear of abandonment; and fear of unworthiness. Most fear nowadays has little to do with our physical survival and everything to do with the latter two, which are at the root of many of these patterns and belief systems.

Most of us are not aware these ancestral patterns exist within us. We have to do deep, sometimes grueling work to excavate the behaviors, thoughts, and beliefs entrenched in our cavernous minds. Can you identify any beliefs you have that may have come from your parents or grandparents? Beliefs around your looks, money, marriage, raising kids, careers, gender roles? Do you complain about or blame your parents for "messing" you up or making you feel a certain way? When you spend your days blaming other people for what you think and feel, you give away all of your power. You may need to spend some time identifying the negative characteristics, behaviors, and/or beliefs you've inherited and forgive them, so you can heal, grow, and create space for new ones!

Here is an exercise you can do to help you through this work. Think of your parents, or any parental/authoritative figures who impact you, as young children. Place yourself in their innocent, little shoes and try to feel what they might have experienced throughout their childhoods that led to the adults they are today. Visualize hugging them and then say something kind, like "You are loved. You are worthy. You are perfectly imperfect, and I accept you just the way you are. You are brilliant and can do anything you set your mind to." This is great to say to yourself, too, when you're in need of a little love. I also highly recommend doing this with the actual children in your life. I say these words to my daughter every night before I put her to bed because I want her to grow up knowing she is a goddess and can achieve anything.

Breaking the Cycle

Breaking the cycle of negative ancestral patterns is challenging, but crucial to your growth and development. Becoming an entrepreneur, even though it was incredibly hard to endure my family's criticism and judgement, was the beginning of separating from my inherited patterns. And when I became pregnant with my first child, I knew I had to declare, "This ends with me." I refused to put my daughter through the same strife my family had caused me, and mom's family had caused her.

Parenting is hard. *Really* hard. It's hard enough, without having to make sure you're not accidentally imparting generations' worth of emotional hang ups to your precious babies. But it is so worth it if you are willing to do the work. My husband Dylan and I both catch ourselves playing out behaviors we've clearly inherited from our parents and grandparents. Through mindful partnership and parenting, we help each other identify, forgive, and heal from these behaviors so we do not pass them on to our daughter.

When I got pregnant, Dylan and I moved from Kansas (where he was from) back to my hometown in Canada. In addition to the normal anxieties and expenses that come from moving, our new apartment cost almost as much as we were making each month. We were *stressed*, and it didn't help that I was supremely sick, all day, every day. One night, we got into a huge argument (I can't even remember what about) and at some point I screamed, "This is just *WHO I AM!*" As soon as the words left my mouth, I felt a pit in my stomach. I instantly knew it was my ego—feeding off an ancestral pattern—talking. Dylan calmly looked at me, with compassion in his eyes, and asked, "But is it? Do you want to be this way? Why are you arguing *for* your limitations?"

I somberly went and sat on the bathroom floor and started to sob. I thought about my family, movies and TV shows, and even encounters I'd had while working in the bartending industry: whenever someone got really mad, they yelled. I'd always assumed that was how everyone processed anger, and never really thought about how it could affect another person. Without meaning to, I'd inherited this habit, but I did not want to pass it on to my husband or child. I kept crying, but my tears quickly became ones of relief and gratitude. I was so thankful to be blessed with a partner who was willing to be brave and confront me on my negative behaviors and beliefs. I decided to forgive myself (and my family) for that behavioral pattern and committed never to yell that way again (of course, Dylan and I are human, so we still argue every so often!). Together, he and I broke that cycle, and I was able to develop a new identity. Now I declare, "No, *this* is who I am, how I behave, and what I do. I am calm and find solutions, instead of resorting to anger. I no longer accept this drama: return to sender with love and consciousness."

Have you ever said, "This is just who I am!" when it comes to some of your less flattering character traits? Chances are good you have, and that's *okay*. It might even be true! But it does not have to remain part of your identity forever and you do not have to repeat the negative ancestral patterns you've inherited. Break the cycle. You get to decide how you move through the world. Once you pinpoint a quality with which you no longer wish to identify, you can develop a new behavioral pattern or standard to replace it. Sometimes this means choosing different words to use or implementing a course of positive action for when the old habit rears its ugly head. Eventually though, with enough dedication and practice, you can reprogram yourself and experience a total transformation.

SOUL WORK

Build upon the affirmations you created in the last chapter to help reframe how you see yourself.

For example, perhaps you've always identified as someone with a short temper. Maybe your father was quick to anger when you were a child. You don't have to continue identifying as a person with a short temper. Try affirming how you do want to behave in moments of anger or frustration.

I FORGIVE MY DAD FOR YELLING AT ME. I AM BREAKING THIS CYCLE. I AM CALM IN THE FACE OF ADVERSITY. I TAKE DEEP BREATHS WHEN I WANT TO SCREAM. I AM THE EMBODIMENT OF SERENITY.

Or maybe you've noticed you judge others' appearances, always noting their weight or outfit choices, because your mother constantly picked apart how you looked (and possibly you've noticed your grandmother does the same thing to your mom!). You can break the cycle by affirming a new identity as someone who uplifts and compliments other people, especially girls and women, with little to no focus on their physical appearance.

I FORGIVE MY MOM FOR MAKING ME FEEL LESS THAN, AND I FORGIVE MY GRANDMOTHER FOR MAKING MY MOM FEEL THAT WAY TOO. I AM BREAKING THIS CYCLE. I AM PERFECT AND BEAUTIFUL, INSIDE AND OUT. I LOVE OTHER PEOPLE EXACTLY AS THEY ARE. I SHOWER OTHER WOMEN WITH PRAISE AND ADMIRATION. I AM GRATEFUL FOR THE GODDESSES IN MY LIFE.

Share your experience online with #IdeaSoulWork

Chapter 7

Remembering Atlantis

When I was eighteen (one year prior to my first encounter with my *Dea*), my mom and I took a weekend class at our Naturopath's academy. The course centered on an energy healing technique called Craniosacral Therapy. The theory is that there is a pulse and fluid that travel in each of our bodies from the third eye, around the skull, and down the spinal column to our sacrum. We were taught how to tap into and feel that energy pulse, as well as how to reset it in order to clear blockages around major energy centers (Chakras). It was fascinating, and opened me up even more to different healing arts.

On the second day of the workshop, we ran into the teacher as we were coming back from our lunch break. We were standing silently at the intersection, waiting to cross the street, when she suddenly turned to me and said, "You had a very powerful past life in Atlantis. You were a healer, and you've come back to heal again."

I was in shock and murmured something along the lines of, "Oh . . . really? Atlantis? Um . . . thank you . . ." I didn't know what to say! She smiled knowingly, and then crossed the street without saying anything else. I was confused, but also intrigued. I hadn't ever really considered whether or not I believed in reincarnation (aside from when my mom mentioned she thought I'd been a witch in a past life). Over the next few days, I kept thinking, *what was she talking about? Atlantis? Seriously? As in, the legendary city that supposedly sank beneath the sea?*

After we finished the workshop, I promptly forgot about what she had said. A year went by. In August 2011, three weeks following my first encounter with my *Dea*, I found myself in the Bahamas.

I was sunbathing by one of the resort's luxurious pools, awash in the warm glow of a humid afternoon, when my teacher's words popped back into my head. *"You had a very powerful past life in Atlantis. You were a healer, and you've come back to heal again."* I hadn't thought about her revelation since the workshop had ended, and I nearly fell out of my chair when I realized: I was at the *Atlantis* Resort.

I believe there is no such thing as coincidence; everything is divinely timed and orchestrated (when you open up to the *Dea*, you will know this too).

An overwhelming tidal wave of feelings came over me: purpose, peace, awe, and excitement. My body started to tingle with intense energy. I'd never told anyone (besides my mom and sister) about my spiritual beliefs or mystical experiences because I'd been afraid people would think I was weird. The sensation I felt was so strong, however, I *had* to confide in someone! A mentor of mine, Ellie, was sitting nearby with one of our colleagues, Mandy, so I blurted out, "I feel like I'm here for a reason, a huge reason, something to do with my purpose, but I don't know what it is!" As I feared, they looked at me wide-eyed and confused, but their shocked looks quickly softened into genuine curiosity.

I proceeded to tell them what my Craniosacral Therapy teacher had told me, as well as about my encounter with my

Dea during my acupuncture treatment, and how it all seemed to be culminating in this magical trip. Mandy, whom I didn't know very well, said, "Did you know I'm a clairvoyant? I have some angel cards in the room. Why don't we have a session tonight and see what comes up?" My jaw dropped to the floor. Of course she was, and I'd been meant to meet her.

To my knowledge I had never known someone who was clairvoyant before, so I was excited to have this new experience and allow myself to open up this part of me in a safe space. She read my cards first. Though the details are hazy now, I remember my cards confirming I was on the right path and that I should keep following my intuition. They also indicated big things were coming and I should be patient, but ready to receive them.

What was even more powerful was when our friend Athena came to the room to have her cards read. Athena had been sick for a few years (she was suffering from kidney disease, but hadn't wanted to miss out on the trip, understandably) and she felt this would be an opportunity for her to receive some guidance about how to proceed with her treatment. As Mandy was explaining Athena's cards to her, I suddenly felt a strong magnetic pull; something was telling me to put my hands on Athena's back.

My Craniosacral Therapy class taught us that when we have a strong urge guiding us to a certain area of the body, we shouldn't resist, but follow the pull. I was self-conscious, worried I would freak Athena out if I asked to touch her. After about three minutes, however, I couldn't take it anymore. "I know this might sound weird but I feel like I need to put my hands on your back. Is that okay?" I asked her. She said yes, so I checked in with my new clairvoyant friend, who nodded her head in confirmation. I placed my hands on

Athena's back, near where her kidneys would be, and felt a massive current of energy flow through the top of my head and out through my hands into her body. I stood there with my hands gently resting on her back, euphoric energy surging through my body, for fifteen minutes. Afterwards, Mandy said to Athena, "You will be alright." She *was* alright, and still is today, over ten years later.

I will never forget that night or the messages I received. The rest of the trip was just as amazing, and I spent the next few days exploring the resort, swimming in the pools and ocean, and bonding with my colleagues. Everywhere I went, I felt a spark of magic in the air. My heart felt fuller and warmer, like the universe was giving me a big hug. A powerful energy surrounded me, always nearby, but I didn't know why.

It would be another five years before I learned what, or rather *who*, was responsible for the sensation.

Sacred Partnership: A Preview for the Coming *Attraction*

In April of 2015, I met an incredible guy named Dylan at my company's annual conference in Las Vegas. We became fast friends and over the next few months, in spite of the fact that I lived in Ontario and he lived in Kansas, we spent countless hours texting and calling each other, plotting our big dreams. Dylan and I came from very different places, but bonded over our drive for success and desire to prove ourselves. We also shared a love for personal development, business, and health and wellness.

As our friendship grew, there was one thing I didn't share with him: from the moment I first met him, I knew, deep down, he would one day be my husband and the father of my children. I knew he was my person, my soulmate, my twin flame, that we were destined to spend our lives together and grow alongside one another. But since most twenty-something guys would get freaked out by that sort of thing, and I'd had tumultuous experiences with guy friends becoming boyfriends in the past, I kept this information to myself until I knew he'd be ready to hear it.

In July of that same year, Dylan and I met in Chicago, where we were visiting a mutual friend. We had a great time—the entire trip was amazing (more on that experience later!)—but even more magic unfolded when I got back home.

The morning after I returned from my trip, I awoke from the clearest, most vivid dream. I was crossing over a midnight blue ocean on a marble bridge, running away from a beautiful city that was bathed in a radiant white light. It wasn't just a dream, though; it felt more like a memory. It was me, but I looked different: I was dressed in a stunning white dress, that looked like the garb of a priestess, and had long and wavy chocolate-brown hair. I knew my subconscious was finally revealing my past life in Atlantis to me.

The next morning, I had the same dream, but an extended, slow motion version. This time, as I was running from the city, which seemed to be crumbling away, I could see a smile spread across my face and my deep caramel-colored eyes twinkling in the moonlight.

Yet again, for the third morning in a row, I had the same dream, but even longer and more detailed: I was running across the bridge; I smiled, eyes twinkling; and then I slowly turned my head to look behind me—I was running *with* someone!

For two more mornings, I was visited by longer, clearer installments of the dream. First, I was running, turned my head, and discovered I was holding hands with the other person whom I *knew* was the love of my life. In the fifth and final dream, after I realized I was holding hands with someone, I looked up and saw him. He had dark, curly hair, a chiseled jawline, the body of a Greek god, and piercing blue eyes, which had a very specific, very *familiar* shape. We knew we couldn't escape the city's destruction, but we both smiled because we knew we would find each other again.

I woke up, breathless and in tears. Without a doubt in my heart or mind, I knew it had been Dylan in Atlantis with me. Our souls wore different bodies and faces, but it was us; our eyes were the exact same, unaffected by the millennia that had passed between the two lifetimes.

Inspired by my dreams (as well as my trip to the Atlantis Resort and the insight from my teacher all those years earlier), I decided to finally start researching the theories, legends, and potential discoveries of the lost city of Atlantis. I watched every video and read any book I could find on the subject.

Note: theories related to many ancient civilizations do not always correlate with historical timelines based on material evidence. Without substantive proof, these theories can be and are often dismissed by academics. My belief is that maybe these are merely missing pieces of our history and as technology advances, perhaps we will finally be able to discover and prove some of these theories about Atlantis and other lost civilizations. The following is my interpretation of the information I discovered, and while it may not be considered "historically accurate," it is what I know and believe to be true. I urge you to do your own research and decide for yourself!

It is my understanding that the first documented mention of Atlantis occurs in works by Plato (the ancient Greek philosopher), called *Timaeus* and *Critias*. Through a series of recounted stories by different characters, Plato alludes to Atlantis having been a real island, home to a technologically advanced civilization, some 9,000 years earlier (the island rested somewhere within the present-day Strait of Gibraltar, the waterway between the Atlantic Ocean and Mediterranean Sea). Atlantis became a great conquering power, but ultimately was defeated in war by Athens, and swept beneath the sea due to earthquakes and flooding (presumably the wrath of the gods). Most people think that Plato's reference to Atlantis is allegorical, a means to warn his Athenian contemporaries against greed and authoritarian control, but Plato always insisted the stories were true.[16]

Atlantis is a legend to which I connect very deeply, but it is one of countless great mysteries of human existence. There have been many fascinating findings all around the globe of unexplainable ancient ruins, underwater cities, and advanced technology that appears to have been invented thousands of years ago. As I mentioned before, I highly recommend you do your own research on what fascinates you. Look into the ancient civilizations of *Nan Madol, Sacsayhuaman, Baalbek, Bimini Road*, and *Dwarka*, to name a few.

We've been conditioned to think we already know everything about our history, which in many cases is interpreted, white-washed, or reinvented all together anyway! Who are we to question the validity of these legendary places? There may be no tangible proof of their existence (*yet*), but absence of proof does not intrinsically mean absence of truth. Even if these stories *are* metaphors, it is important to honor them as lessons from the Universe, passed down to us through written and oral tradition. There is knowledge to glean from the story of Atlantis, whether it's an historical truth or renowned fable. Atlantean civilization fell because of greed, war, and an insatiable desire to conquer others—sounds like the human masculine, doesn't it? An unbalanced patriarchy that has lost touch with the Divine?

The dreams I had after visiting with Dylan in Chicago enlightened me in ways I never could have anticipated. I knew Atlantis had been real, and I had lived there. I knew I had loved Dylan in that past life. I knew my former world's demise was caused by a disconnection from Divine energy. And I knew my purpose in this lifetime was to help my new world avoid a similar end by helping people, particularly women, heal their relationships with their inner goddesses. Before I could start down that path, however, I also knew . . . I had to tell Dylan about everything.

When Dylan and I officially started dating a year and a half later, I finally shared everything with him. I told him about Atlantis, my deep knowing of his soul, and that we had a mission to fulfill together.

As our love intensified and we continued to share every single detail of our lives with each other, we discovered Dylan had been on that same trip to the Bahamas. He'd been swimming in the same pools and eating at the same restaurants. I hadn't realized it at the time, but the cozy, loving sensation I'd experienced while on that trip had been Dylan's Divine Masculine energy connecting with my Divine Feminine.

Chapter 8

Falling in Love with *Me*

"How you love yourself is how you teach others to love you." - Rupi Kaur (Poet)

Like so many little girls, I always dreamed of one day finding my Prince Charming. When I was twelve years old, I got my first "boyfriend." I'd been bullied a lot as a kid, so finally having a boyfriend felt like a huge triumph. After a month, however, I realized I didn't want a boyfriend! I liked being independent, so I broke up with him. The other kids went back to bullying me, including my "ex" and his friends, who made me their number one target when we played Dodgeball in gym class. Afterwards I would wait for everyone to leave the girls' locker room and cry my eyes out, nursing the bruises on my body—and my ego. Before I'd even really hit puberty, I found the notion of relationships to be bleak and hopeless. And yet, in spite of the traumatic experiences of my youth, I desperately craved to be loved by someone.

I didn't have another boyfriend, or my first kiss, until tenth grade. I proceeded to have a few relationships throughout high school and college, but most were extremely toxic. I was cheated on, lied to, and treated like an afterthought. By the time I was nineteen, I decided not to pursue any serious relationships and strictly dated casually for three years as I built my businesses, went out with friends, and focused on personal development.

One thing I learned during that time that had a profound impact on me was the concept of the six needs. Several personal development experts have expounded on this idea, though I personally learned about it from Tony Robbins.[17] Basically, every human has six needs, and the people and situations in your life will usually reflect which of those needs are currently most important to you. The four "human" needs are: certainty (feeling in control, having a routine, knowing); uncertainty (variety, spontaneity, surprise); love and connection (with others and/or yourself); and significance (feeling good about yourself, recognition, edification from others). The two "soul" needs are: growth (feeling progress, steps forward, working on ourselves, difference); and contribution (giving back, helping others, making a difference). The six needs can apply to relationships, business, health and fitness, etc.

Your current life situation will generally mirror the needs you value most at any given time. For example, if you feel stuck in a job you dislike, it might be because your two top human needs are "significance" and "certainty." You may have a set schedule, which gets you home at the same time every evening, and have gotten a raise or promotion recently, which validates your career choice. And yet, you hate what you do because these needs are based on logic, and not emotional or spiritual fulfillment. You might feel brave (or fed up) enough to walk away, should a better offer come along. But let's say, in addition to the schedule and salary, your boss always tells you what a great job you're doing and you really like your colleagues. This would now satisfy "significance" and "certainty" as well as "love and connection," which means three out of your four human needs are met. Chances are good, you won't leave that job—even if something intriguing comes along that could help you attain one or both soul needs. It's important to understand which needs are most important to you and identify which areas of your life are meeting them—and which ones are not.

I became obsessed with the soul need of "growth" (still am!). I was sick of feeling stagnant in my life and craved forward movement in my health, my entrepreneurial endeavors, and my self-love. I forced myself to get out of my comfort zone. I devoured books about money and finance, and built my businesses with integrity and intention. I attended trainings and seminars, and actually implemented the lessons I learned (this is *key*). I cut ties with toxic people and surrounded myself with positive humans who were on their own personal development adventures. I traveled all over and learned about other places and cultures. I explored my artistic side and started painting. I became plant-based, choosing to fuel my body with healing nutrients from nature. I exercised, with a focus on body positivity and not perfection. I honed in on the patterns and behaviors that weren't serving me, and developed soul-nourishing rituals: I woke up early; drank tea; meditated; practiced gratitude; pulled from angel cards; and visualized my happiest, most abundant future. My *Dea* and I were having the time of our lives!

I went another four years without any romantic or sexual entanglement. This period of my life was my "self-love revolution." It was about becoming *my own* one true love— *not* about changing myself in order to find a better boyfriend. I didn't worry about looking for a new relationship because I was too busy falling deeply, madly, and unconditionally in love with myself.

"Raise your standards and the universe will meet you there."
- Danielle LaPorte (Author)

If your standards are low, that's what you will manifest. If you have not taken the time to heal from the belief that an abusive spouse is normal, then chances are good, that is the sort of partner you will attract. If you feel like you are doomed to suffer from unrequited love (something with which I struggled), you will be in a vibration of unworthiness, and you won't be able to call in someone who likes you back. Maybe you are setting standards that are so high, you are actually self-sabotaging every potentially awesome date because you keep finding something "wrong" with them. The focus cannot be on perfection—the perfect person doesn't exist, but the perfect person for *you*, in all their imperfect glory, is far more likely to come into your life when you commit to operating at your highest vibrational frequency. We all have different romantic standards based on our families, friends, past relationships, personal morals and values, and life experiences, but you have to be crystal clear—and optimistic—about the person you want to attract.

Though I wasn't actively seeking a relationship, I did decide to get very clear on my standards for what I would want in a life partner, *just* in case he decided to show up one day. I described my ideal boyfriend/husband as someone who: believed in true, radiant, unconditional love; valued growth and hard work; would never let me compromise my values; lifted me up emotionally and spiritually; made me laugh; could have fun in any situation; was open-minded; and made me feel safe (not just physically, but also mentally and emotionally). I filled my vision book with journal entries describing imaginary dates and conversations he and I would have (and *maybe* a picture of Zac Efron, though specific looks didn't really matter to me). I read through my vision book nearly every night for years, trusting that if this person existed, the Universe would deliver him to me (and in the meantime, I would be blissfully content being alone).

All of the work I did during those seven years of being single led to the awakening of my inner goddess. At a certain point, I had fallen so completely in love with myself (and my *Dea*) that I honestly thought we might not ever really need a romantic partner for fulfillment. I had set very high standards for my life and refused to settle for a partner who wouldn't match those expectations, even if it meant being single forever. But I *also* had faith that the higher my vibration, the more likely I was to find that perfect mate.

SOUL WORK

Begin to fall in love with yourself. Make a "self-love list" by writing out all of the things you love most about yourself— no judgement, no perfectionism. If this is hard for you, ask your partner/best friend/sibling/trusted mentor to tell you five things they love about you, and then build your list from there. Then write out all of the qualities you aspire to have or develop, and pick the top two or three you think will best help you get to that "next level." Go to your favorite online or local bookstore and find a book related to building those character traits.

If you need help getting started (after you finish this book, of course!), visit AwakenDea.com and check out the list of some of my favorite personal development books!

Share your experience online with #IdeaSoulWork.

Chapter 9

Sacred Partnership

His name was Dylan and we met on Instagram.

He worked for the same health and wellness company and as soon as I saw his profile picture, I knew he was the one. I actually ran upstairs, screaming with excitement, and proclaimed to my sister, "I found my future husband!" Every post made me fall more and more in love with him. He was wise, shared the same beliefs about life and business, and even wrote poetry. Although I had imagined someone like him for years, I still couldn't believe someone so handsome, smart, and philosophical actually existed. Eventually we became virtual friends and started sending each other direct messages, which resulted in exchanging phone numbers so we could text and call each other.

And then he got a girlfriend

In the past, I would have been destroyed, but since I had been doing so much personal development and was in my flow, I trusted everything would work out the way it was supposed to. A few months later, as the Universe would have it, they broke up, which led to him going on his own journey of self-love discovery. We talked and texted often, helping each other through various personal and professional difficulties. Sometimes, though, he would take days or weeks to respond to me. It drove me crazy, but I trusted my *Dea* and had patience—for nearly one whole year.

As I mentioned in Chapter 7, Dylan and I first met in person at our company's annual conference in Las Vegas. He came to meet me at my hotel and I thought the anticipation was going to make me faint: my whole body tingled and shook; my palms were drenched with sweat; and I had to keep reminding myself to breathe. When I finally saw him walking into the hotel lobby, I went into a trance-like state. The world slowed down and blurred, save for the two of us. He was taller than I expected, so I had to look up into his (strikingly handsome!) face. When our eyes connected, there was a magnetic pull—I couldn't look away, even though I was flush with nerves. I thought, *I know those eyes. I've known you for thousands of years, and I've finally found you again. I'm home.* What I actually said was, "Hey! So good to finally meet you!" (not exactly the first words you imagine saying to your soulmate, but oh well). We chatted for a while, excited to finally be in the same room after spending so much time getting to know each other from afar.

Our first encounter, while magical, was brief—I'd actually been on my way out with some girlfriends, who started dragging me to the taxi queue. Dylan followed me outside, the two of us still conversing as though no one else was around. I barely noticed being shoved into the cab. As I looked out the rear window, desperate to catch one last glimpse of him, I asked the Universe to have him turn and look at me so I would know he felt our Divine connection too. Slowly, he turned around and our eyes locked—an electric current surged between us, our gazes connected by an invisible power line. That night, while my friends partied in bars and nightclubs, I returned to my hotel room, blissfully "high" from my intoxicating first encounter with Dylan.

The conference only lasted three days and since Dylan and I were on different teams, we spent most of the time sitting apart from each other—in a giant arena, filled with 16,000 other consultants. Even in the vast sea of people though, I could spot him within moments. Our connection was so strong, his aura would explode just for me so my eyes would be drawn to him.

In between conference events, we made a point of seeing each other as much as possible. On one lunch break, Dylan invited me to his room so we could catch up away from the noise of tens of thousands of excited consultants. We laughed and flirted and took our first picture together. Other times we grabbed food with mutual friends, sat by the fire pits at my hotel, or walked and chatted hurriedly before another session started. Every moment left me more and more enamored, and I flew home from that conference with my head literally and figuratively in the clouds

After Vegas, I started working more with my spirit guides. One day I did a meditation during which I received three gifts from three of my guides. The first two gifts were a yellow flower and a music box that would only play music that made me feel good. My third gift was a vibrant, violet-colored stone. After presenting it to me, my guide said, "When you receive this sign in the conscious world, it will signify something very important in your life." I didn't tell anyone about this experience.

In July, I met Dylan in Chicago, where our mutual friend Kailey lived. Before I got on the plane in Ottawa, I called my best friend and told her I was setting the intention that if he aligned with my spiritual beliefs and we could connect deeply beyond physical attraction, then I would know for sure he was "The One." I had no idea what Dylan's spiritual/religious beliefs were, but I knew I had to find out on this trip.

I wasted no time. I knew Dylan could end up thinking I was a "woo-woo weirdo," but I had to risk it in order to find out if he really was my soulmate. On our first night together, I did angel card readings for Kailey and Dylan. Since Dylan seemed so open, I also told them about meeting my inner goddess and shared stories about my guides (I didn't tell them about my most recent "gifts," however). In turn, Dylan recounted some past life experiences he'd recently had through meditation. I couldn't believe it—he *did* believe in the same things as me!

The three of us spent hours that night sharing and bonding. At one point, when Dylan and I were alone in the kitchen, he said, "Sammi, I didn't know you were so spiritual. We have so much in common to talk about." I was ecstatic and spent the rest of the trip looking for more signs that would confirm our spiritual destiny. I was ready to justify the faintest flicker of a sign, but what I received was a brilliant sky illuminated with fireworks.

One afternoon we were driving through the Illinois countryside, just outside of Chicago, and we passed a field full of yellow flowers. During that same drive, all of my favorite songs spontaneously played on the radio. My guides' first two gifts had shown themselves!

At one point during the trip, Dylan and I decided to perform Reiki healing on each other. Reiki is a healing art form, during which you allow pure energy to flow through you in order to heal the other person. It doesn't require any physical touch, just an open heart and pure intention. I moved my hands slowly over his body—from his feet to his lower chakras to his heart. As my hands hovered above Dylan's chest, I felt an explosion of energy. It felt like I was going to float away or be blasted into the wall, so I firmly planted my feet and closed my eyes. Every inch of my body started to vibrate at a supersonic speed, forcing me to open my eyes so I could make sure he was okay. At the same time, his eyes flew open—he looked stunned. "Do you feel that?!!!" he exclaimed. "YES!!!" I replied. There was intense, overwhelming magic in the room.

On our last night together, I guided Kailey and Dylan through the same meditation I had recently done. Afterward, they both described their guides and what gifts they'd received. When Dylan disclosed his, my jaw dropped to the floor. "My last gift was very interesting," he said. "It was a bright purple stone." Kailey, who noticed my mouth agape with wonder, asked if I was okay. I assured her I was because I didn't want to divulge that I had also received a purple stone from my guides. I worried Dylan would be freaked out or think I was lying, but I knew what it signified: we were supposed to be together.

I already told you about the dreams I had about Atlantis after returning from that Chicago trip, as well as the subsequent research I did on the mysterious lost civilization. What I didn't tell you was that during my research, I came across the "lost stone of Atlantis." My heart nearly burst when I clicked on a link that took me to an image: a striking, fuchsia-colored stone. The caption beneath the picture of the stone talked about the ascended master Saint Germain, and how he was responsible for bringing twin flames from Atlantis back together on Earth, to help raise the planet's vibration. When I did a deep-dive into Saint Germain, nearly every image depicted him with an amethyst-like stone pendant around his neck and a violet aura around him. I started to cry. Everything—our spirit guides and their gifts, my Atlantis dreams, Saint Germain—was pointing me to Dylan.

Occasionally, both during and after the Chicago trip, Dylan would become withdrawn and feel resistant to connecting with me. It was confusing how red hot and then glacially cold he could be, but I trusted the Universe was testing our Divine selves by reminding us of our humanness, and I trusted that my *Dea* was guiding me down the right path.

Months later, Dylan and I got to reunite in person as mentors at a teen leadership camp in Toronto. There was *a lot* of connection (and palpable sexual tension) between us, which became obvious to everyone around us. The other mentors and people running the camp would ask us if we were together, but of course—we weren't. It pained me to have to say, "No, we're just friends…" over and over again, but I had faith and trusted the Universe's process.

On our last night in Toronto, my roommates were partying and I couldn't sleep. I texted Dylan, who invited me to sleep in his room (he'd been given private accommodations since he'd also been the keynote speaker for the camp). As I walked down the hotel hallway, hyper aware of how quiet everything seemed, my nerves overtook me. I inhaled deeply and asked my *Dea* to keep me calm, collected, and grounded.

We tucked in for the night, hugging our respective edges of the bed, and turned off the lights. Instead of falling asleep, we started talking. We asked questions, told stories about our childhoods, and confided our fears, hopes, and dreams to each other. We got closer and closer—emotionally and physically. After about an hour, the tips of our noses were grazing, and I could feel Dylan's cool breath on my forehead. Nervous energy compounded into a ball of fire and desire in my stomach, and a slight smile crept across my face. This was it—our first kiss. The same fireworks I'd felt in Chicago turned into a blazing inferno of lust and passion. We hit a boiling point and melted into each other (while still respecting one another's boundaries). The intense connection we had while kissing (*just* kissing!) was more sensual and transcendent than any other physical experience I'd ever had.

Unfortunately, by the next morning, Dylan had resumed his "hot and cold" routine. While I felt light, free, and drawn to him, he seemed tense, closed, and distant. He avoided me all day, which was especially confusing since he was supposed to be coming with me to Ottawa for five days.

When we quietly boarded the train the next day, faced with a five-hour ride together, he turned to me and said, "We should talk about the other night. I don't know if we're meant to be together and I don't want to ruin our friendship. I respect you too much and I only want to move forward with 'The One.'"

My stomach flipped and I immediately felt devastated, but luckily my goddess took over and reminded me to proceed with strength and serenity. I said, "I go with the flow and know I'll end up with the perfect partner I'm meant to be with."

If that ended up being Dylan, I trusted the Universe would provide; and if it didn't, I was not about to make myself feel small because he'd "rejected" me. My *Dea* helped me understand that Dylan was behaving out of fear of committing to the wrong person, and had more work to do on himself before he could feel ready to commit to *me*.

Fear of commitment is so common, especially in my generation. Most people fear commitment (to a relationship, kids, new job or business, house, etc.) because they think it will cause them to lose their freedom or feel trapped. But the purpose of having a relationship is to grow alongside another person, which can only happen if both souls are willing to engage in a long-term commitment. Love blossoms from the growth we experience through shared challenges— not from running away at the first sign of hardship. You have to be willing to face the deepest holes and darkest corners with the other person. I realized Dylan simply wasn't ready to do that with me until he was certain about us. I actually respected him for being honest and for being so committed to finding the right partner. After all, I hadn't wanted to get into a relationship unless it was "The One," so I couldn't possibly expect him to commit when he wasn't sure.

The train ride was smooth sailing after that conversation. All of the stress and expectation we'd been feeling disappeared, and we were back to laughing and feeling comfortable with each other. Every so often he would touch my knee, and my *Dea* would giggle and assure me, *Just wait. He'll change his mind—and soon.*

Two nights into his visit we fell asleep in my bed while watching a movie. I awoke the next morning to the most magical, tender kiss. Divine love and warmth surged through my body every time he touched me. I maintained a deep knowing that even though it wasn't the right time for us, he would come around. And so, our journey continued.

A year after we'd first met in person, we once again found ourselves at our company's annual conference in Las Vegas. I could tell he was still feeling resistance towards me (but I also recognized he was in the midst of some deep, grueling personal growth work). To compound the mixed signals he was sending, he invited me to visit him in Kansas that summer. Of course, I accepted.

When he picked me up from the airport, he immediately told me he'd met his soulmate at a recent seminar. The playful butterflies fluttering in my tummy transformed into jagged, heavy boulders. I held back tears, told him I was happy for him, and spent the rest of the day making small talk with him.

Before bed I locked myself in his bathroom and had a chat with myself in the mirror. As I looked at my face, I realized I couldn't see *me*. I was wearing a mask of makeup and was pretending to be the kind of girl I assumed he wanted. I decided in order to honor myself and my *Dea*, and in order to be totally honest with Dylan, I had to strip away the veneer and stop playing a part. If he wasn't going to be with me, it was going to be because he'd seen every piece of me and made an informed decision. I washed away all of my mascara, foundation, and lipstick, as well as my feelings of insecurity and unworthiness. I traded my cute, flirty pajamas for sweatpants and a hoodie, and stopped worrying about what my body looked like. I vowed to myself and my *Dea* that I would spend the next week as my authentic self. *If he really likes me, I'll know he likes the* real *me. And if he can't like the real me, I don't want to be with him anyway.* It was hard for me to admit, because I knew in my heart we were meant to be together, but I had to release the human masculine desire to force things to work and trust in the Divine.

When my *Dea* and I emerged from that bathroom, glowing with confidence and pride, Dylan just stared at me. *Oh crap, he thinks I look bad without makeup,* I thought. *But if that's the case, it's his loss.* Instead, he said, "Wow. You look *really* beautiful without makeup, Sammi." I smiled, and we went to bed.

Because Dylan was a gentleman (not to mention infatuated with someone else), he crashed on the couch and let me sleep in his bed. We got to know each other even better as friends, laughing, eating out, and visiting with his parents and brothers. I'd never met them before (other than his mom, briefly at our business conference), but I immediately felt like I belonged in his family. It was a wonderful, platonic visit, and I returned to Canada knowing I'd stood in my power, as my true self. I detached from the outcome and moved on with my life, free and happy.

Part of moving forward meant worrying less about Dylan and recommitting to my personal growth and business endeavors. I hired a coach, who gave me all kinds of incredible advice and guidance about life, business, and love. During one of our sessions, he was explaining the concept of Agape love, which is the highest form of devotion—soulful love for every human, animal, and inch of this earth and universe. He taught me that when you practice Agape love, you are fully authentic and free to express who you are and how you feel.

I asked, "Do you think I should tell Dylan how I feel then?"
He took a deep breath and proceeded to tell me the most incredible story.

There was a woman, who lived in New York City, who waited for true love her whole life. When she finally found the man of her dreams, she was too afraid to tell him because in the past, her feelings had always gone unreciprocated. For months, she wanted to profess how much she loved him, but she let her fear overpower her. One Tuesday morning in September, she received a phone call from the man. He told her his office building had been hit by an airplane and he didn't think he would make it out. He told her how deeply he loved her and how he wished they could have been together. In shock and disbelief, she told him how much she loved him before they lost their connection. She vowed from that day on, she would never withhold love from anyone, ever again.

My coach said, "Samantha, does it make sense to withhold love from the person to whom you want to give it the most?"

Tears streamed down my face as I realized what I had to do. I owed it to myself to be honest about my feelings with Dylan. How could I not, after hearing that story? After two years, it was time to show up for me (and my goddess) and finally share my deep knowing about our destiny with the man I loved. The Universe had waited long enough, and I didn't dare wait for another sign, in case it never came.

I was absolutely terrified. My hands were shaking when I finally picked up the phone to call Dylan, and it took me another twenty minutes before I actually pressed the call button. As the phone rang, I sat on my bed and tried not to hyperventilate. When he answered, I started talking immediately—I didn't want to give him a chance to say anything that would derail me from my purpose.

"Dylan, I haven't been honest with you and I need to be. I need to be authentic to myself. It doesn't matter what you say or think afterwards, but if I don't express this to you, I'm doing both of us a disservice. From the moment I knew you existed, I have felt a deep love for you. I can't explain it, but I have this strong knowing that you are the one for me. For the past couple of years, it has only grown stronger and stronger and I can't ignore it. It comes from within my soul. It doesn't matter what you feel, I just had to be honest with you." I rambled on like this for a while because I was nervous about how he would answer, but finally I stopped talking and allowed him to respond. He said he felt similarly, but still wasn't one hundred percent sure and needed more time. We already knew we were going on a mission trip to Central America together in March, and agreed he would give me his decision then. I didn't mind waiting because I knew with time, he'd have the clarity to see the truth about us, and I could spend the next few months feeling more free, powerful, and Divine!

It only took him six weeks.

Out of nowhere, Dylan called me and said he couldn't stop thinking about me and finally knew in his heart and soul that I was the one for him. It would be three more months before we went to Guatemala for our mission trip, so we decided he should come to Ottawa before then.

Before he arrived, we talked every day, for hours at a time. We made an agreement with each other that officially dating meant this was it—we were each other's forever, and would eventually get married and have children. We were entering into a sacred partnership, which meant we were each other's priorities and would never stop growing, personally and as a couple. Dylan and I vowed to hold each other to our highest selves—to always honor our inner god and goddess. When one of us was not acting in alignment with our Divine power, the other would call it out. He and I were all in—body, mind, and soul.

When he came to Ottawa in January, we made the decision to get spiritually married to each other. We held a private ceremony, for just the two of us, during which we set our intentions to love, learn, and grow with each other forever.

It took nearly three years for us to come together. For three years, though we battled with our human selves, I maintained faith that Dylan and I were destined to unite when the timing was right. It was like a fairy tale, but instead of a prince in shining armor saving a damsel in distress, there was a radiant, confident goddess who shined so brightly she was able to find her soulmate. Together, they became twin flames, bonded in sacred partnership.

SOUL WORK

Whether you are currently in a relationship or looking for love, there are powerful actions you can take to make your intentions clear, and strengthen your connection with your significant other *or* help you call in your ideal partner.

If you are currently in a relationship:

Write out everything you love about your relationship, as well as areas in which you would like to grow (some examples might be more dates or different types of dates, making dinner together, agreeing to put your phones away at a certain time, taking time each day to talk without any distractions, reading a particular book together, going to couples therapy, splitting up the household chores, etc.). Ask your partner if they are open to doing the same, and then create a safe space in which the two of you can share your lists. It's cliché, but true: communication (open, honest, safe communication) is key to a healthy relationship. Promise you will really listen to each other and *hear* what the other person is saying, without getting defensive or waiting to respond with what *you* want. Check your egos and show up as your Divine selves. Afterwards, create a relationship vision together. You could even make a vision board or book! I highly recommend you go through this exercise every few years (or even months) depending on what has changed in your lives as individuals and as a couple. Remember, a relationship is a continuous work in progress, but the more you communicate and come together in harmony—with a goal of mutual growth—the more fulfilling and fun the "work" will be. If for any reason your partner can't or won't participate, I encourage you to do this exercise on your own—it will still help clarify things for you!

If your partner is willing, here is a way to take it one step further. Sit across from each other and look directly into each other's eyes for as long as you can. Silently or aloud, forgive each other (and yourselves) for any resentment or pain that's been festering, as well as any traumatic incidents that happened in your collective past. Try to see beyond the flaws or past mistakes, and look into each other's souls until you really see one another's divinity and feel pure love. Some deeply rooted emotions may arise, but once you feel them, see if you can acknowledge, forgive, and then release them.

For a more in-depth experience, visit AwakenDea.com and check out the "Sacred Partnership" meditation, which you can listen to *with* your partner!

If you are seeking a relationship:

Write out all the areas in which you'd like to grow, or personal qualities you'd like to improve upon, in order to show up better for your next relationship. Then do the same exercise as above, but with yourself in a mirror. Look deeply into your eyes and forgive everything you see as having been wrong in your past relationships—forgive yourself *and* your past partners. Next, write out all of the qualities of the next version of you, the you who will be in alignment and ready for love to appear. Finally, write out everything about your dream partner and relationship—don't be attached to the who or the how, just trust that everything you desire exists in someone out there. Remember, you will attract someone who aligns with where you are and who you are being, so keep developing into the best version of yourself!

Share your experience online with #IdeaSoulWork.

Chapter 10

Embracing Your Cycle

A few years ago, I was sitting in a coffee shop with one of my dear soul sisters. Per usual, our conversation quickly shifted from making small talk to digging into deeper issues. Sometimes we talked about our love life or businesses, personal development journeys or new amazing books we were reading, but on this particular day, we somehow found ourselves discussing our periods.

Menstruation is treated very differently depending on where you live or to what culture you belong. For example, the Cherokee Nation reveres women's cycles, and considers women who menstruate to be powerful and sacred. Several Native American and indigenous cultures believe that periods signify "when women [become] goddesses connected to the moon."[18] There are several cultures that provide women with special places for them to stay while they menstruate, in order to allow them to disconnect from their daily lives, bond with other women, and be in touch with their bodies, nature, and Divine Power.

Unfortunately, this great respect for women's cycles is more often the exception, and not the rule. In some places, due to lack of access to feminine hygiene products, girls are unable to attend school and thus receive less adequate education. Various cultures regard a woman with her period as dirty and impure. In Nepal, though it has been deemed illegal, they often still practice *chhaupadi,* which is when women are confined to menstruation huts because they are considered tainted. Tragically, many women have died as a result of this custom.[19]

Much of colonized, capitalist, "western" culture has stigmatized menstruation as well, making it taboo while simultaneously turning it into a multi-billion-dollar industry. In 2019, the Feminine Hygiene Products Market was estimated at $26 billion, and is expected to surpass $37 billion by 2025.[20] And of course, most of that profit is shared by giant corporations, owned and managed primarily by men. This is clearly illustrated by the marketing for feminine hygiene products, which typically implies a period is an annoying, smelly, messy, painful nuisance. The solution? Products filled with chemical dyes and fragrances, bleach, and loads of other toxic ingredients harmful not only to women's bodies, but also the planet. But if we buy them, we will no longer be foul and unclean so . . . problem solved, *right*?!

The human masculine, in fear of the Divine Feminine, has managed not only to profiteer off our sacred cycles, but also somehow make us feel bad about them. We're told our wild mood swings and overly emotional tendencies make us ill-suited to hold political office, run major companies, or generally behave in a way suitable to the patriarchy (but we know that's not true, right goddess?!).

All of this information fascinated and inspired us, and the more research we did, the more we knew we had to help women develop better relationships with their periods and bodies. It was time for a Menstruation Revolution! In the coffee shop that day, we started writing an outline for a course. A few days later, my friend channeled and downloaded intricate details about what we should share from her own *Dea*. Within a few weeks, we'd booked sessions with fellow goddesses who were also ready to renew their attitudes toward, and connections with, their beautiful, natural cycles.

During our first women's circle, I was entranced by the Divine Feminine magic of the women around me. Complete strangers were opening up and connecting. These women were healing deep wounds and resentment toward their femininity, right in front of our eyes. We watched each woman release pain, step into her *Dea*, and expand with Divine energy (if you've ever seen the animated film *Moana*, I liken the experience in that room to when *Te Fiti* regains her heart and transforms from a lava monster into a beautiful, vibrant goddess of the Earth). I felt so blessed to have the opportunity to share space with these soul sisters.

Every month, we have the opportunity to physically shed what no longer serves us and welcome in a new cycle of "birth" or creation. When we connect to our bodies' internal cycles, we can utilize our energy in very productive, natural ways. There are rituals you can adopt into your life that will help you honor your cycle and learn how to ride these waves of energy (not unlike the moon impacting the tides!). Amazingly, sometimes through this work your menstrual cycle will wind up aligning with the phases of the moon. And if you do not have a menstrual cycle, for whatever reason, please know you are an equally powerful, awe-inspiring goddess who can harness the power of the moon's cycle to create magic in your life.

Fun fact: when we first started doing this work, our cycles were synced with each other, as well as the full moon. Over the following year, both of our cycles switched to the new moon. It's especially interesting because within a year of starting our goddess circles, she and I both got pregnant and gave birth to our sweet girls. Aren't our bodies incredible?!

Cycle Ceremonies

There are three goddess archetypes that align with the different phases of life, as well as the moon. The Maiden represents the waxing moon, embodying youth, new beginnings, expansion, and enthusiasm. The Mother represents the full moon, embodying fertility, fulfillment, sexuality, and power. And the Crone represents the waning moon, embodying wisdom, truth, honor, and endings. Depending on your phase of life and where you are with your cycle, you may connect with one of these three goddesses more than the others.

If you currently experience periods, use your natural cycle as a guide for the following rituals. If you don't experience periods, use the moon's cycle (you can also do both, if you like, in order to have extra magic throughout the course of a month!). You can adapt these practices in any way that feels authentic to you and resonates with your Divine energy. Don't worry yourself by trying to be perfectly in sync, either— the intention behind the process is what truly counts!

There are four phases in each cycle: the rise; the seed; the dive; and the shed.

THE RISE PHASE: end of menstruation – ovulation / New Moon – Full Moon

This is a time for creative energy, socializing, and productivity. You may feel more extroverted. Set your intentions for the creation phase, which is next, and see a clear vision of you in your power, with your divine *Dea* glowing from within.

During this time, work on your passion projects, connect with new people, and call in new opportunities. This is the best time to attend social events and networking gatherings. You may feel called to try new things, like attend a yoga class or join a meetup group that practices a language you're learning. Whatever your heart and intuition pull you toward, trust and follow it! You and your *Dea* are creating magic in this phase!

Possible affirmations to use during the Rise Phase: I AM OPEN TO NEW EXPERIENCES! I AM CREATIVE AND ENERGETIC! I AM WELCOMING NEW OPPORTUNITIES FOR THE BEST POSSIBLE OUTCOME! I AM A DIVINE GODDESS WHO IS PRODUCTIVE AND ALIGNED WITH MY GOALS!

THE SEED PHASE: during ovulation / Full Moon

This is a time to plant the seeds of intention for what you want to "birth" into your life. In terms of a menstrual cycle, this is when the egg is released; if fertilized, it can grow into new human life. Whether or not you are trying to conceive a child, attract a promotion, build a new business, create a new work of art, start a project, etc., you can energetically use this phase to set an intention of "birth" or creation. Get really clear on visualizing your desires and then release them to your goddess; she knows the best way to transform those desires from energetic to physical forms. It is not your job to figure out how things in your life will manifest; desire and visualize them with as much specificity as possible, and then release them, trusting that your *Dea* will bring them to you.

During this time, honor your body with a soothing self-care practice, like drawing a bath with rose petals, essential oil (vanilla and/or lavender are great), candlelight, and soft music. Visualize the "birth" of what it is you want to create as you quiet your mind and release tension from the day.

Possible affirmations to use during the Seed Phase: I AM CREATING A BEAUTIFUL LIFE! I AM READY TO RECEIVE [*INSERT YOUR BIG DREAM/INTENTION/GOAL HERE*]! I TRUST MY INNER GODDESS TO INCUBATE MY INNERMOST DESIRES AND DREAMS! I SURRENDER ANY RESISTANCE AND TRUST IN DIVINE TIMING THAT MY DESIRES WILL MANIFEST!

THE DIVE PHASE: from ovulation – menstruation / Full Moon – New Moon

This is the time when you will want to dive more deeply into yourself and become more introspective. You might feel more emotional, be in need of rest, and desire time alone/feel more introverted. By drawing inward, you can focus on what you will want to release during the next phase in order to create space for a new cycle.

During this time, be gentle with yourself, and make time for additional pampering and self-care. If you do not journal regularly, this would be an ideal time to sit with yourself and write about anything you've kept bottled up or that hasn't been serving you. You may even want to hang on to it so you can burn it/dispose of it during the next phase! The Dive Phase is also great for working on things "behind the scenes." Rather than being out in the world promoting and networking, you may want to spend this time building out systems and fine-tuning details.

Possible affirmations to use during the Dive Phase: I AM IN TOUCH WITH MY INNERMOST SELF! I TAKE CARE

OF MYSELF AND TREAT MY INNER GODDESS WITH RESPECT AND LOVE! I AM RELEASING WHAT NO LONGER SERVES ME! I FILL MYSELF UP FIRST IN ORDER TO OVERFLOW AND GIVE MORE TO OTHERS!

THE SHED PHASE: during menstruation / New Moon

Now is the *period* of time (get it?!) when you can physically, emotionally, and mentally release all that no longer serves you. In terms of menstruation, this is when the body sheds the uterine lining because there is no fertilized egg to protect.

Take what you wrote during the previous phase or write a new list of everything you want to shed. Be as specific as possible. For example, if you wrote down, "I'm letting go of fear," try to go deeper and get very specific. Fear around what? Perhaps you've been holding yourself back in your business because you're afraid of sharing your products or services. Rework your intention: "I am letting go of fear around selling my products/sharing my services." Maybe you want to shed self-doubt, anxiety, or poor body image. Once you've gotten super specific, set the intention to discard these old feelings, doubts, and worries in order to make space for the new. If you like, and it is safe to do so, you can burn the paper (or shred/tear—whatever works for you!). However you choose to get rid of these self-limiting beliefs, focus on really *FEELING* them release and leave your mind and body. Visualize and feel the new space being created that will allow for new beliefs and ideas to flow in.

Possible affirmations to use during the Shed Phase: I AM LETTING GO OF FEAR AROUND [*WHATEVER YOU'RE*

109

AFRAID OF! I AM SHEDDING THE OLD ME SO MY INNER GODDESS CAN SHINE THROUGH! I AM MAKING ROOM FOR NEW POSSIBILITIES IN MY LIFE!

As you move through these four phases, monitor the changes in your thoughts, feelings, and energy. Do you feel more introverted, or outgoing, at certain times? Maybe you notice you always need a nap during your Dive Phase? When you pay attention to your personal cycle, you can begin to take advantage of when you're feeling more productive, when you need rest, when you should start new projects or do something creative, when you should schedule dates with friends, etc. Instead of being angry or frustrated with your body, you can learn to go with the flow and allow each phase to help you connect more profoundly and intimately with your Divine Feminine power.

For example: as I write this, I am sitting on my couch, curled up in a blanket. I can feel menstrual cramps coming on, and my lower back is sore. And yet, I feel grateful because I know I am about to begin my Shed Phase. I welcome every ache because I honor my body and the miracle it is performing. Because I know where I am in my cycle, I can set appropriate intentions and administer some self-care.

SOUL WORK

Evaluate your current attitude towards your menstrual cycle. Do you dread it? Embrace it? Do you track it? Consider using an app or keeping a calendar to monitor your period in order to learn more about yourself, your body, and your connection with the moon!

Additionally, look into shopping for feminine hygiene products from small, woman-owned businesses that offer safer, non-toxic, organic, or sustainable options.

For more resources on cycle ceremonies and goddess circles, visit AwakenDea.com!

Share your experience online with #IdeaSoulWork.

Chapter 11

Motherhood

Your *Dea* doesn't look for anything outside of herself to create what she wants. Think of it like Mother Mary, who birthed a miracle without any seed from a man or any outside force or help. She had divinity within her. Perhaps Mary was a goddess, sent to signify the rising of the Divine Feminine, but humankind allowed patriarchal dogma to reign supreme and Mary merely became the conduit for a miracle—no longer the miracle herself. It seems as if the human masculine cast her aside to be a supporting player: the vessel for new life, but not life itself. And yet, in several religions and belief systems, even outside Christianity and Catholicism, Mother Mary is celebrated as a goddess, an ascended master, an enlightened being, and an angel. Regardless of what we believe to be true, we can all be inspired by Mary—you too can create a miracle from within your Divine self. I believe I have birthed amazing miracles with help from my *Dea*, but none have been so extraordinary as my first daughter.

I've already told you a bit about Dylan's and my rollercoaster love story. I could say we never experienced any ups and downs once we finally got together, but of course that would be far from the truth. In spite of Dylan and I having a fairy-tale-like origin story, we have had to continue to grow and learn and make space for one another in our lives. There have been plenty of bumps in the road, and we've had to do a *lot* of work to honor the vows we made to each other.

113

Two months after getting spiritually married, we went on our mission trip to Guatemala to work with orphanages and schools. I remember one day, I was cuddling this sweet baby girl, and Dylan and I were smiling and laughing, talking about how we'd have babies of our own someday. We talked a lot about our future on that trip—travel, marriage, me moving to the United States, kids. We decided we would ultimately have two children and would travel the world together as a family. Dylan and I discussed where we would live, what additional businesses we'd start, and soul-nourishing projects we'd create (like writing books!).

For several months, we traveled back and forth to see each other and planned our next great adventures (we were determined to spend a couple of years abroad, traveling around the U.K. and possibly living in Australia for awhile). We'd *finally* gotten together, and were making up for the years of tension and separation. And then, while I was visiting him and his family in Kansas in the spring of 2017, my period was late. *Five days* late.

It can't be, I thought. *We've been so careful.* We'd diligently planned around my cycle, which I'd been tracking carefully since starting the goddess circles.

"Except that one time," I said aloud, as I sat on the toilet with a pregnancy test in my hand. Dylan was on the bathroom floor, leaning back against the wall, tensely running his fingers through his hair. We were both shaking with nerves as I followed the test's instructions. We were sure in two minutes it would all be over: the test would be negative and we could resume our plans for world travel and domination.

It didn't even take the allotted two minutes. Within a few *seconds*, I was staring at a giant blue plus sign. The shaking worsened and I started to cry as I showed Dylan the positive pregnancy test. A cyclone of emotions overtook us: fear, delight, sadness, joy, and grief, for the life and dreams we'd been planning. My masculine "doing" energy took over: I thought about all of the logistical plans we'd have to make, like moving Dylan to Canada so we could have the baby in my home country (universal health care!). I started babbling about every detail but Dylan embraced me, calmly, and said, "It's going to be okay. We will get through this. Obviously this was meant to happen. There must be a little spirit who wants to join our family."

Of course he was right! I had to trust Divine timing and my *Dea*, who'd never steered me wrong. I took a deep breath, calmed down, and smiled: we were going to be parents! We'd created new life through our love and passion for one another.

We emerged from the bathroom in a daze and took refuge in the living room, to relax a bit before Dylan's family came home. All of a sudden, his mom—who had *just* left—burst in through the front door and exclaimed, "What's going on?! You're pregnant!" She had been driving out of the garage when an intense *knowing* came over her—she could feel what we were discovering at that very moment!

I was gob smacked. "How did you know?!" I asked her through tears.

Christy pulled me and Dylan into a group hug and said, "You two are so powerful. You will figure this out, and everything will be okay." And I knew she was right. I trusted her instincts, since she had spent years awakening her own goddess and learning how to trust in the Divine.

Dylan and I took turns freaking out and being at peace, but eventually we both came to fully accept and rejoice in what was about to be our greatest adventure yet.

Mother-goddess instincts swelled up in me quite quickly. I envisioned a vibrant, easy pregnancy and a beautiful, effortless water birth in a tub at a special birthing center. I became very protective of the precious life growing within me and decided I would eat cleaner than ever—only fresh fruits and vegetables, ideally straight from our garden whenever possible. I would load up on nutrients from Mother Nature herself, to keep me fueled as I became a mother too. All of that lasted for about five days, and then I was sick—all day, every day, for the following nine months.

For weeks I lied in bed, unable to move without throwing up. The slightest motion, like getting up to use the bathroom, would have me violently purging what little food I'd been able to keep down. To make matters worse, in my first trimester I got the worst sinus infection of my life. My nose was clogged, which made breathing while getting sick very complicated and at times, very scary (once I basically had to give myself the Heimlich Maneuver on the edge of the toilet to dislodge something caught in my throat! Not exactly the radiant-goddess-creator-of-new-life image I'd concocted when I first found out I was pregnant!).

Through it all, Dylan was amazing, compassionate, and luckily not one bit squeamish. He watched me devolve from a passionate, glowing, energetic goddess to a miserable, fragile, sick mess. He held my hair when I threw up, ran me baths and showers, and made me food, even though I usually couldn't handle eating anything. Because I was so sensitive to movement, I couldn't handle cuddling or touching, which put a strain on us. I desperately wanted to connect with him physically, but my body was too busy being nauseated all the time. My stomach, as well as my heart and soul, were emptying of all energy and emotion. About eight weeks into my pregnancy, after a particularly horrendous night of puking, we decided to go to the emergency room.

I was diagnosed with "Hyperemesis Gravidarum," also known as severe morning sickness. They gave me two bags of fluid through an IV, as well as anti-nausea medication. I was resistant to the meds at first, because I'd wanted to have as natural of a pregnancy as possible. I'd grown up visiting naturopaths and acupuncturists, so it made sense I'd follow suit with one of the most important health-related journeys I'd ever take. I reflected on how awful I'd been feeling, which had prevented me from enjoying being pregnant and sharing any excitement with Dylan and our families. I didn't *feel* like a goddess anymore, but I trusted my *Dea* to guide me; *she* told me to trust the Universe, which was currently offering me a solution. I knew I had to surrender to the process. It would be silly to refuse out of pride or some goal of having a "perfect pregnancy" (which doesn't exist—every pregnancy is a unique miracle with its own appropriate, and usually unpredictable, course of action).

With the help of the meds, I eventually started to feel well enough to emerge from the basement bedroom in Dylan's family's home and spend some time on the couch in the living room. I hadn't worn makeup or clothing outside of pajamas or sweats in over two months. I felt like more a troll-goddess emerging from her damp, dreary cave! On one particular morning, the hot sun of a midwestern summer

117

streaming in, I was reading a book, blissfully unaware of the events that were about to unfold.

Dylan came into the living room holding a beautiful white lace dress. It was stunning, long and flowy—a total goddess gown. My stomach rumbled but, for the first time in weeks, with *happy* nerves. A tingling sensation went up and down my spine and limbs and I swear my jaw hit the floor.

Oh my goodness. This is it. I know what's about to happen. I was speechless.

Dylan looked at me with loving, careful eyes and sweetly said, "Go take a shower, do your makeup and hair, pamper yourself, and put this on. You have an hour."

My eyes lit up with love and excitement as I took the dress from him, gave him a kiss, and went to our bathroom to get ready. I reveled in each moment of those sixty minutes as I primped and prepped. In the shower, I could feel every droplet washing away the previous weeks' worth of sickness. I was cleansing my body, but also my mind and soul; I was on a mission to feel pure and fresh for the future. I couldn't stop smiling! As I did my makeup and curled my hair, I gazed at myself in the mirror, looking at the *Dea* within. Deep in my eyes, I could see flashes of my life— every moment that had led me to this time and place. Before I finished, I called my sister and assuredly said, "Dylan's going to propose today!"

I walked back upstairs, refreshed and rejuvenated. I finally felt like the goddess I had been before being consumed with morning sickness. *If nothing else happens today, I am still so grateful to Dylan for helping me feel like my old self again*, I thought as I climbed into Dylan's car. As we drove, he held my hand and played all of our favorite love songs. *But I just know it's going to happen!*

"Where are we going?" I asked coyly.

"Just for a drive," he responded. "You'll see."

We drove into the country and I felt like the car was hovering above the road, like we were floating on a cloud of love. Twenty minutes later, we pulled up to an idyllic little house, replete with a wrap-around porch, geese and chicken, and lush vegetable and flower gardens—some of which boasted flowers taller than me! A sweet-looking woman emerged from the cottage. She welcomed us and then guided us down a path, through the storybook-like property, until we arrived at a large canvas tent. She bid us farewell and disappeared into the verdant grounds.

Dylan took my hand and led me inside the tent, where I discovered a table and chairs set for a picnic and a big bed surrounded by twinkling fairy lights. On the bed were pictures of Dylan and me throughout the years, as well as a handwritten note. I delicately picked up the letter and read Dylan's beautiful message to me as tears streamed down my face. When I finished reading, I turned around to give him a hug but found him down on one knee, hands extended, holding a beautiful ring. I held my breath as he shared his deep love for me and then, after what simultaneously felt like an eternity and a single second, he asked me to be his wife.

That evening, we enjoyed a delicious dinner on the porch of the house. Dylan's mom and brother surprised me by serving us our meal—in aprons and everything! When they weren't spoiling us with amazing food, they sneakily took pictures from around the corner. The whole meal was filled with love and laughter, and afterwards Dylan and I enjoyed a romantic campfire and gazed at the stars in the big, jet-black sky.

Newly engaged, we packed up our belongings into Dylan's Ford Focus and drove for three days back to Ottawa. Poor Dylan had to drive the entire way because my anti-nausea medication made me extremely tired (and constipated, if you were curious!). I tried to be a good passenger, but for most of the trip I was a useless zombie.

Once in Ottawa, we had a lot of work—and growth—to do. We were about to get married, had a child on the way, and had never lived together in our own place. This abrupt change in our life plan was actually a powerful gift. It forced us to evaluate how small we'd been playing, how limited a scope we've had of our potential. We hustled, and within two weeks, secured a nice apartment in the best part of town.

On the first night in our new home, our first as a couple, we ate vegan pizza on a picnic blanket on the floor while Dylan worked tirelessly from his phone and laptop, trying to achieve a huge milestone in his business. We didn't have any furniture, our mattress was on the floor, and there was barely any food in the cupboards yet, but it was such a special night. Dylan hit his business goal, and the next chapter of our lives officially began.

We didn't want to wait until after our baby was born to get married and since I didn't want to be "showing" during the ceremony, we decided to get married right away. Since we were on a tight deadline, both came from very large extended families, and had very little financial resources, we opted for an intimate affair with our immediate families, grandparents, and a few friends. Two months after we got engaged, on a perfect summer day in Canada, we found ourselves getting married in my mom's beautiful backyard garden.

The ceremony was a perfect reflection of who Dylan and I were. We did it our way, without fuss or stress. Dylan insisted on being barefoot, so he could be grounded. We created a circle of rocks into which we ceremoniously stepped to signify our new life together. The day was about us and our love, and it was everything I ever could have wanted for my wedding.

Birthing the Mother

"No one ever mentioned it—in nine whole months, not one person said, 'You're about to meet someone entirely new. And it's not your baby, it's going to be you.'" Fourth Trimester Collective[21]

Pregnancy was a catalyst for growth and transformation for me. It was not easy or comfortable, and although I felt so grateful and blessed for our baby's and my good health, it challenged me in ways I never could have predicted.

It was hard to stay positive while dealing with the never-ending morning sickness. It kept reminding me of traumatic childhood experiences when I would feel sick to my stomach because of bullying; often the anxiety got so bad, I would throw up. Every morning before school I would clutch the sides of the toilet, sure I was going to be sick, sobbing as my parents stroked my hair and assured me I would be okay. I was determined not to repeat that cycle of anxiety and depression during my pregnancy, but knew it would require

121

a commitment to increased self-awareness and difficult inner soul work.

Many (if not most) physical ailments can usually be connected to some sort of spiritual imbalance. After five months of constant puking and nausea, I did a deep dive into what the purging might be symptomatic of on emotional/mental/spiritual levels (obviously morning sickness is a very real and common physiological side effect of pregnancy, but in my gut I knew there was more going on). What I evaluated was my tendency to get violently sick usually happened when there was a sudden change in my life. Past instances included when I experienced bullying and when I lost my grandfather. This time, it was obviously activated by my pregnancy and all of the swift life pivots that came with it. I knew my *Dea* was telling me to purge what no longer served me in order to rid my body of dark energy and create space for new light.

While a child is in the womb, they absorb our energy, thoughts, and emotions. I became very intentional with my time and energy, focusing on rest and self-care. I learned how to say no more often, finally realizing I wasn't obligated to do things I didn't want to do (I will forever be grateful to my daughter for helping me finally learn this lesson!).

I'd also been holding on to toxic friendships that were plagued with passive aggressiveness, guilt, and burden. These relationships were weighing me down and creating a lot of inner turmoil. My body was energetically tied to so many people, all over the world, many of whom were not positive influences. The knot in my stomach became a metaphor for the entanglement of connections with people whom I did not want impacting my child. I knew I needed to bless and release.

I did a lot of "cord cutting" and forgiveness practice during my pregnancy, so I could move on from relationships that would not be healthy for me or the family I was creating. Sometimes this looked like unfriending people on Facebook or unfollowing people's social media profiles; in other cases, I stopped agreeing to help people with things when they weren't putting in any effort themselves. I made a conscious decision to stop expending precious energy on people who couldn't show up for me, but even more so—show up for *themselves*. I distanced myself from those who were caught in a low-vibe loop of victimhood, blaming, and complaining. I broke the cycle of people-pleasing and codependency, and set new standards, so I could teach my daughter what beautiful, enriching, soul-nourishing friendships could and should look like.

Life wasn't about just me anymore. It was about creating a bright, beautiful future for my family unit—me, my husband, and our baby—unencumbered by unhealthy patterns. In order to do this, I had to reconnect to my goddess in a new and even more meaningful way. This meant going inward, enveloping myself in a cocoon of self-love and harmony, preparing myself—body, mind, and soul—for the strenuous metamorphosis that would happen at the end of the nine months. I meditated every day, listened to hypnobirthing programs, plastered affirmations all over the apartment, and became very aware of and connected to my body. Each day I would extend my personal development work to my baby. I would hold my belly and speak directly to her, saying things like, "You are so loved already!" and "We can do this together!" and "We can't wait to meet you!"

Before I gave birth to my daughter, *I* was reborn. I realized how powerful I was as a woman and how much I had to offer the world. I met a new version of myself, and she inspired me to work harder, go farther, and become more than I ever thought possible. When it came time to give birth, the new version of me, with the help of my Divine *Dea*, felt as ready as we could be.

Dylan and I were sure the baby would come early; his mom even came to stay with us two weeks before our estimated delivery date just in case. We waited and waited. At two weeks *past* her due date, we were no longer eligible to go to a birth center, as we'd planned. We were disappointed, but trusted the Universe's plan.

For days I'd get contractions, but then they'd stop. We tried *everything* to jumpstart labor. I walked six to ten miles every day on the treadmill. I even took castor oil, a common "last resort" for many mamas. We went out for Indian food on the eve of forty-two weeks of gestation. After the spiciest chana masala I'd ever had—*still* no movement in sight—my midwife informed us I would need to be medically induced the following morning.

I lied in bed that evening and Dylan and I prayed to Saint Germain for help and guidance. I meditated and tried to ease into rest, but then I had to pee for the millionth time that evening. I got up, went into the restroom, and suddenly felt a bursting sensation. WHOOSH! The dam had broken and a rushing river of fluid flowed from me.

"Dylan!!!" I yelled. "My water broke!!!"

Dylan and his mom raced in and we all stood and stared at our baby girl's first signal that she was finally ready to meet us.

CRASH! The three of us jumped at a loud bang that had come from the living room. When we entered the space, we discovered the painting I'd done of Saint Germain had somehow flown off the wall and traveled *halfway across the room!* True story! Dylan and I looked at each other in amazement as we explained to Christy how we'd just been praying to Saint Germain for assistance. In that moment, with complete faith that everything was going to be fine . . . contractions started again.

My contractions were still relatively far apart, so we went back to bed to try to get a good night's sleep before the real action started. But at around 1 a.m., I woke up and felt nothing. She still wasn't ready, but I had complete faith in her Divine timing

After being medically induced at 9 a.m. the next morning, I spent thirteen hours in high intensity labor, experiencing extreme contractions every minute and a half, lasting a minute and a half each. I was able to labor in the tub, using my Hypnobirthing techniques to help me through the intense surges. I entered a trance-like state during those thirteen hours, moving through each rush with focused breathwork and meditation. For more than half a day, I was in the zone, going with the flow, a total badass. But my body had been through so much already, and I started to shake uncontrollably. Every time I had a contraction, the baby's heart rate would plummet. The midwife checked my dilation and I was still sitting at four centimeters (and I needed to get to ten before I could push!). A knowing came over me and I sensed my *Dea* guiding me through the process, sending

125

me a crystal-clear message: although it had not been part of my birth plan, it was time to get an epidural.

The intensity was overwhelming, and if I didn't get some relief through the next phase of labor (I knew it could be another twelve hours or more before the baby came), my body would shut down due to all of the additional hormones pumping through my veins. The doctor administered the epidural, and it was *incredible*. I lied down and fell asleep, my body succumbing to the rest it so desperately needed.

Our sweet baby girl entered the world after twenty-two hours of active labor. When my arms finally cradled her tiny, perfect body, tears of joy fell down my face. I loved her before I knew her, but I never could have predicted the immense, overwhelming, awe-inspiring intensity of the love I felt in that moment. We were both healthy and back home six hours later.

I wish I could say everything was perfect from the moment we crossed the threshold of our apartment, but for the sake of transparency I don't want to end the story there. Too often during my pregnancy I read stories about picture-perfect homecomings, peaceful babies, and connected partners, and I felt extreme pressure to make sure our baby girl's first day with us was calm and uneventful. That is not always the true story or full picture, however. Though having our baby was the most amazing, life-changing experience and was so, so worth every pain-staking moment, it was also stressful and scary. As soon as we got home from the hospital, Dylan had a massive panic attack and I started to meltdown.

We've survived pregnancy and childbirth, but what now?! How do we move forward knowing we are now responsible for this precious little life? How do we keep this child, our child, alive?!

I felt so stressed and tired from nearly a full day of intense, painful labor I could barely see straight, let alone be supportive of Dylan. We were so blessed to have help from Christy, who offered to watch over our girl so we could take a nap and regroup.

When I awoke from my nap, though still suffering from absolute exhaustion (a fatigue that ached all the way down into my bones), all I could feel was joy, love, and gratitude. We were now a family of three connected spirits, united on this earthly plane, and here we were, together in our first home, enveloped in pure, unconditional love. I craved more sleep but all I could do was lie on the couch and stare at my sweet little baby's face. I gently ran my hand across her little forehead and down her teeny pink nose, caressing her soft and delicate head covered in peach fuzz.

Dealing with an infant wasn't easy, but we steadily found our footing as new parents. Becoming a mom and dad presented so many new tests and obstacles to overcome, both as individuals and as a partnership. It was the most painful, glorious, difficult, wholesome, exhausting, and rewarding experience of our lives, and we are challenged by these new roles each and every day. Like all dualities in life, it is a hard, but beautiful blessing and we continue to learn and grow through the process.

As I write these words, our baby girl is two years old. She is the light of our lives—the blessing that rocked our world, and then changed it for the better. She has been the ultimate reminder that there is beauty in adversity if you choose to

127

have a positive mindset and look for ways to grow and thrive when presented with life's greatest trials.

A message to all my fellow goddess-mama-warriors: I see you, I feel you, I honor you. Motherhood is *hard*. Many parents go through dark periods after the arrival of a new baby, and I do not want to ignore how difficult the aftermath can be, even when things go "perfectly." There are crazy cocktails of hormones gushing through your body, you feel overwhelmed and sleep deprived, and sometimes you can't connect with your partner the same way (we'll cover that in the next chapter). Postpartum Depression is an overly stigmatized, but very common condition that can range from mild to extreme (if you're struggling with PPD, please seek help—I included a resource below*).

When Motherhood starts to feel like too much, please—be gentle and kind with yourself. Forgive yourself for not meeting society's expectations of being "perfect." Forgive yourself for the choices that didn't pan out, the plans that had to change. Forgive yourself for slipping up, falling down, or becoming disconnected from your Divine power every now and again. Your goddess is always there for you.

And if you're not a mother, don't want to be a mother, couldn't become a mother, or did not physically birth your precious babies, please know I see and honor you too. You are also a goddess-mama-warrior, who is Divine and powerful and able to nurture and birth all sorts of wonderful things. As women, we can bring life into conversations, friendships, romantic relationships, businesses, art, and so much more. We can care for our siblings, parents, friends, colleagues, extended family, pets, and even plants (and of course, ourselves and our inner goddesses!). When we plant seeds of love, passion, acceptance, greatness, and love, new life blossoms in all sorts of exciting and magical ways.

*POSTPARTUM **SUPPORT** **INTERNATIONAL**: 1.800.944.4773 ~ postpartum.net ~ support@postpartum.net

Chapter 12

Sacred Sensuality

In Regena Thomashauer's book *Pussy: A Reclamation*[22], she discusses the reclamation of the word "pussy," as well as the Divine Feminine. Regena has studied intimacy and feminine power throughout most of her life and this masterpiece of a book contains the knowledge she has acquired. Her teachings helped me reawaken to the Divine power of my body after it had served as an incubator, a passageway, and a source of nourishment for my daughter for almost two years. It was hard to see my body as a living, breathing, wondrous temple, but *Pussy* aided me in the process of feeling like a woman again, in addition to being a mother. A lot of the book challenged me and made me uncomfortable, but I realized that was the point: to get out of my comfort zone, reprogram how I viewed sex, and get my proverbial groove back (I highly recommend it for all goddesses!).

The discomfort I felt while reading *Pussy* is so common, especially amongst women. Particularly in North America, there is a hypocritical need to suppress female sexuality and, taking it a step further, make women feel ashamed of their bodies and sensual natures. Sex should not make you feel dirty, embarrassed or shy (though if you feel any of those things when thinking/talking about or even having sex, please don't feel *more* embarrassed! This is a process!). We've been conditioned to repress our natural desires because the patriarchy (human masculine) is terrified of a world in which women own their bodies, minds, and raw, Divine power.

Sex can be a sacred, transcendent act that honors the Universe and the Divine, and yet most of us have a warped view of it. And why wouldn't we?! Talking about it in any sort of real, authentic way is taboo and yet sex is all around us, everywhere, all the time, generating unrealistic expectations of what it should look or feel like—and what *we* should look or feel like doing it.

The unrealistic, manufactured images of women's bodies used in marketing are designed to make you feel shitty about yourself so you'll buy whatever product they're hocking. Social media and photo editing apps have added to the noise, making us feel like we have to look a certain way in order to be beautiful. The reality is, very few women look like the models and actresses in these advertisements because most of us don't have butt implants, breast augmentations, surgically lifted cheeks, lip fillers, botox, hair extensions, false lashes, veneers, acrylic nails, spray tans . . . the list goes on and on. There's no shame if you happen to want or have any of those things, but you should ask yourself two very important questions: are you altering yourself because it will help you feel personally empowered and because you really want it, or are you doing it because you think you need to change something in order to be beautiful?

We need to be more realistic about how certain looks are attained so girls and women can stop hating themselves every time they open a magazine, turn on the TV, or scroll through social media. There is a fine line between enhancing and embellishing our natural beauty and completely altering the amazing goddesses we are in the name of looking "perfect" for a society that profits off our low self-esteem and insecurities. My wish for my daughter, for all girls and women, is she will be able to look at her face and body and realize how perfectly imperfect she is—that every wonderful bit of her is unique and magical and Divine.

Men endure similar pressures too. They're expected to be strong and unemotional, work out endlessly until they attain a chiseled, muscular body, be excellent at sports, make tons of money, have a luxury car and an expensive house, and—for extra points—be able to serenade with a guitar.

All of this stems from a superficial, capitalistic lie that we must look and act certain ways in order to attract a mate.

The obsession with porn and "hookup culture" has made it so there is very little reverence for sex anymore. I'm definitely not a prude, nor do I personally believe you have to wait till marriage to enjoy the pleasures of sex, but I am disheartened by how disillusioned society is when it comes to sex. This sexual cynicism has permeated younger generations too, sadly. Social influences, changes in hormones and puberty, and the desire to be "cool" generate so much pressure to be hyper-sexual at a young age. And we don't spend nearly enough time educating young people about their bodies or sex in a sensitive, thoughtful, reverential way.

We as parents need to be more mindful of our kids' struggles and beliefs so they can feel confident when it comes time to make good choices around sex and physical intimacy. The "birds and bees" conversation won't be uncomfortable or shameful if we don't make it that way, but rather center it on safety (emotional and physical), empowerment, reverence, and self-respect.

I want to teach girls (and grown women who need it!) to respect and love their bodies. To honor their femininity. And to hold their sexuality sacred with intention and love. I want to help them awaken their inner goddesses, to know they don't need anything or anyone outside of themselves to feel validated or powerful or like they belong. I want young girls to learn about meditation and mindfulness and self-love, and show them how to uplift and inspire other goddesses.

I want all this for boys, too. I want to teach young men to have respect for girls, but also for themselves and each other. To be able to hold space for each other and not be afraid to be soft, sensitive, or emotional. I want boys to learn to protect and honor women, without patronizing or demeaning them; for them to hold sex in high regard, and show up fully not only for their romantic partners but *all* their relationships. I want the next generation to unearth their Divine power and learn how to balance their masculine and feminine energies. To love and uplift one another, regardless of gender, sexual orientation, race, religious beliefs, age, family life, economic position, or popularity status.

Imagine celebrating your unique beauty and being more real, raw, and open to embracing your imperfections. I want nothing more than for you to love yourself just the way you are and to see your innate splendor, the same way you see unblemished beauty in newborn babies. When I look at my sweet daughter, all I see is perfection. As I watch her grow, I keep thinking, *How could she possibly get any more perfect?* And then she does, because she is so completely, confidently herself.

Goddess, I want you to see yourself in this way. Let your beauty shine and please don't ever feel like you owe the world, or anyone, a different version of you. When you can do this, you can start to embrace the sensual being you are.

Whether you identify as a ravishing seductress or a nookie novice, a swinging single or a happily married mother of five, you can choose to embody your sensuality at any time. Goddess, it is time to set yourself free! Pleasure is a door to your power and it can be mined or created in many different ways, with or without a partner. From time to time, I get a strong urge to paint. It becomes an irresistible impulse, a random itch out of nowhere I just have to scratch or else I feel like I might explode. This creative drive helps me connect with my Divine Feminine energy and release any blockages I'm experiencing—personally, professionally, and sometimes even sexually.

Discover what allows you to feel liberated as a sensual woman. Find ways for you to express, release, and engage with that part of yourself. Maybe you treat yourself to a candle-lit bath with essential oils and rose petals. Maybe you read an exciting book. Or maybe you blast some music and dance—with or without clothes! You could give yourself or your partner a massage, during which you kiss and show appreciation for every inch of your/their body. You could spend a quiet evening cooking your favorite decadent meal. Or you could spend a wild night having the steamiest sex of your life! Don't judge your instincts; just have fun and get excited. Whatever feels good, do it—and then do *more* of it! Slow down, lean into pleasure, and try to release any resistance or self-consciousness you have around expressing your sensual side.

Healing Intimacy

Sometimes, even after you've done a lot of personal development and healing work, you can still carry a lot of baggage when it comes to sex. I had spent years focusing and working on myself, *for* myself, but still had a lot to work through when it came to being physically intimate with another person—even Dylan. He and I had tons of sexual chemistry, a magical physical connection, but I was still very triggered by sex when Dylan and I started dating. We had to talk about our intentions and create a sacred space for sex between us. The two of us even gave our love-making a new name ("merging") that more accurately reflected the soulful exchange we were having: a bond that transcended the physical mechanics of sexual intercourse. This new word more accurately reflected the deep love, reverence, trust, honor, and respect that emanated from us when we were intimate.

Once we got over the initial hurdles, we freed ourselves to explore the unknown, experiencing bliss and ecstasy beyond what we knew possible. Our sex life was better than I ever could have imagined; or at least that was the case, until I got pregnant.

Because I suffered from such horrific morning sickness throughout most of my pregnancy, I could barely tolerate any sort of movement or touching. As you can imagine, that put a tremendous strain on Dylan's and my relationship. We were still so young and vital, and yet our intimacy had unexpectedly come to a screeching halt. I could derive no pleasure from sex due to my illness, and to complicate matters, my libido took a nosedive after baby arrived. Dylan was incredibly patient and understanding, but I still felt guilty. I made an occasional effort to be physical with him, but instead of being romantic, sex felt more like a chore.

It was a very confusing time. I closed up and didn't feel as open with Dylan anymore. He hadn't done anything wrong; in fact, he'd been amazing. He made me feel loved and cared for, comfortable and protected, but I just couldn't connect with that part of myself anymore, which made it impossible to connect with him. I actually started to backslide into my old programming of thinking a man will do whatever it takes to get what he *really* wants. Even though Dylan never behaved in a way that warranted it, I started treating him as if he was some sleazy guy at a bar trying to get in my pants. He'd say, "I am your *husband*! I love you more than anything and I want to connect with you on every level." I knew that was true, but my brain kept betraying me. I'd get so mad at myself for not being able to show him love the way I wanted to.

Since we are both solution-oriented people, Dylan and I buckled down and did our research.

We learned about the five love languages, a concept explored and popularized by Gary Chapman.[23] The five love languages are words of affirmation, acts of service, receiving gifts, quality time, and physical touch. Dylan and I hoped that by figuring out how we prefer to give and receive love, we could possibly find some common ground and slowly make our way back to deeply passionate intimacy.

I found that most women feel more connected, open, and safe when they are in tune with their partner emotionally, mentally, and spiritually. If it is only a physical connection, women will not generally feel deep love for or safety with their partners. Most men feel primarily connected through physical intimacy, as it is a time for them to release tension, pressure, and stress. So women find it difficult to get turned on when they feel stressed, but men need sex to release

137

their stress—sounds like a recipe for disaster, right? It was no wonder Dylan and I were struggling!

Based on a study with over 20,000 couples, David Schnarch, PhD found that 26% of couples had sex once a week, while the majority of couples only had sex once or twice a month, and sometimes less.[24] Now of course, every person and every couple is different and there are myriad reasons for not having sex. Sometimes, sex is not necessarily a priority for other couples the way it was for me and Dylan—and that's okay! But love/connection *is* one of the six human needs, so it's not surprising that so many people who don't experience regular physical intimacy struggle to feel fulfilled and happy in their relationships.

During this time, I also talked to other moms and long-time married folks. I was relieved when I realized our problem wasn't unique—or permanent—and as a result, it didn't have to feel scary. In fact, it was important to have a sense of humor about it whenever possible! I attended a leadership meeting during which we were discussing ways to balance our work and home lives. One leader explained her "72-hour rule." She explained that "after about 72 hours with no sex, men get cranky, irritable, and crabby." We all laughed uproariously, but I appreciated her point. Tending to your partner's needs, whether through regular sex or better communication or helping around the house more, is crucial to keeping harmony within a relationship. I was encouraged by all of the advice I received during this time; it helped me understand that our disconnection wouldn't last forever if Dylan and I were patient and kept working at it.

Cultivating your relationship is like going to the gym. You can't sign up for a membership and then say, "Well! That's done! Now I am fit and healthy!" and then go home and sit on the couch all day. Playing video games won't magically give you washboard abs simply because you belong to a gym. You have to make the time to *go and work out*. You have to exercise consistently, sometimes for weeks on end, before you can see results. Gyms and relationships should come with the same disclaimer: "Effort Required."

Sometimes (often) that effort looks like open and honest communication. If your relationship is worth fighting for, like it was for me and Dylan, then you have to *talk things out*. We had so many intense conversations during that time, hashing out fears and worries, and getting in touch with how the other person was feeling. We would acknowledge when we felt disconnected and ask for the time and space to sit and talk so we could get to the root of the problem.

Dylan and I applied this not only to intimacy, but to all aspects of our relationship. We were committed to our growth and getting back to a deep, passionate love. We focused on gratitude, and started sharing what we were thankful for in each other, instead of nit-picking all the time. One of our rules became, "If it won't matter in five years, don't spend more than five minutes on it" (we weren't able to track down who came up with that advice, but we found it so helpful!). We would even sit down and discuss what new habits we wanted to develop together—as a family, in our relationship, *and* in the bedroom.

I emerged from that postpartum period of life a more confident, more empowered, more sensual goddess because I allowed myself to move *through* the problem, instead of ignoring it. I reclaimed my sexuality and you, dear goddess, deserve to feel the same way!

Additional Guidance

If you are experiencing something similar in your partnership and are wondering where to start, here are some guidelines that have worked for me and Dylan.

Every time there is disconnection in our marriage, it is because one of us isn't allowing ourselves to be vulnerable—fully seen and heard. When this happens, we know it's time to get uncomfortable and strip down—mind, body, and soul.

If there is a lack of flow in your intimate life, you and/or your partner might have blockages that need to be cleared, or baggage that needs to come to the surface, for healing. Emotions from old wounds or past trauma (like infidelity, for instance) that have been festering can manifest as physical ailments. Women often hold pain in their lower chakras, many times symbolizing an unhealed emotional wound surrounding love, sex, and/or intimacy (we'll explore this in the Soul Work section below). For example, I would experience various pain or discomfort in my pelvis and tailbone or have irregular pap tests and biopsies (that ended up being absolutely nothing, thank goodness, but these were still uncomfortable and traumatic experiences). Everything pointed to my past pain connected to sex.

The first step is to create a safe space with your partner so you can both open up fully and feel courageous enough to be deeply vulnerable. This requires an agreement from both of you: you are each willing to set your ego aside, show up with love and trust, and really listen to each other without getting defensive, resentful, or putting up walls. Sometimes these conversations can take hours to get through, but if you're both committed to the process, the time will be well worth it. Holding space for each other to do this work (that most people avoid!) will make your bond stronger, but it will take practice, emotional awareness, and pure intention.

The most powerful way to do this is to sit comfortably facing one another and hold hands. Look into each other's eyes for a few minutes and remember *why* you chose this human to be your person. Take turns opening up, giving one another a chance to share fully without interrupting or commenting. This isn't the time to dispense advice, but to *listen*, without prejudice or opinion. When you don't understand something, ask a question, but don't accuse or judge. Remind each other you are showing up as sacred partners to move through this together. Have compassion and grace for what they divulge, which will often have very little to do with you or your current relationship. Give them the safe space to release their pain and emotions. Cry, hug, kiss, keep holding hands—whatever feels authentic and true to the moment.

Once this phase feels complete and you both feel lighter, free from the constraints of previous painful relationships or sexual trauma, agree to forgive and then set your intentions for the next phase of your partnership. You may establish a schedule for date nights or create a relationship vision board together—whatever feels right for you! However you choose to map out your relationship, sit together and plan it all out. Yes, even your sex life! You may choose to create a new name for your love-making, or work on reprogramming what sex means to the both of you. Spice things up and raise the vibrations in the bedroom (pun intended). Communicate and compromise until you've made a passion plan that feels good to both of you.

Repeat as needed! Just remember, goddess: you deserve to enjoy sex that is transcendent, magical, and spiritual. It can be an amazing experience with the right person, the right energy, and the right intentions.

SOUL WORK

It's time to release any shame or negative feelings you've been carrying from a relationship or sexual/physical/romantic encounter that is no longer serving you.

DISCLAIMER: If you have been through any kind of physically or emotionally violent trauma, you can absolutely still do this exercise but I strongly recommend therapy or counseling (and legal help if necessary). Getting help is a practice of self-love.

If you feel called to, set your scene with some meditation music, turn the lights off and get cozy. Lie down and close your eyes. Visualize a glowing light around your body—this is your aura, and we are going to clean it up! You may see strings coming off the back of your aura in different places, which symbolize past experiences from which you need to heal—cords that need to be cut. The strings will be in different places around you/your aura depending upon which chakra (energy center) they've attached to.

If it was a sexual encounter, the strings may have attached to your root chakra (near your tailbone/pelvic floor, associated with safety and grounding) or sacral chakra (near your belly button/lower belly, associated with sensuality and creativity). If you've been feeling like someone took your power from you, or you gave your power away, the cords might be attached to your solar plexus chakra (between the bottom of your ribs, in the middle of the torso, associated with personal power and self-esteem). Or perhaps it was a love relationship; in this case, the strings will probably be affixed to your heart chakra. In matters of miscommunication, or being prevented from speaking your truth, there might be strings near your throat chakra. And if it was a situation having to do with spiritual energy or clarity (or lack thereof), your third eye (on the forehead, between your eyebrows) or crown (just above your head) chakras may be cluttered.

Identify any strings or colors that aren't reflective of your pure, radiant aura. Then visualize a beam of light streaming from the top of your head and down your spine. Allow this light to cut through all of the strings and impurities attached to your aura. See the strings wither away, shrivel up, and disappear. Allow that piercing beam of light to shine all around your body, spotlighting and then cleansing anything bogging you down. Do this until you can see your aura glowing and shining brightly on its own again. You should feel lighter, clearer, freer. When you do, open your eyes.

Share your experience online with #IdeaSoulWork.

Chapter 13

Transcending Shadow Archetypes

Archetypes are universal "characters" we act out in our lives that reflect common traits from which we tend to model our everyday patterns or behaviors. Carl Jung, the psychiatrist, famously talked about archetypes and how they've formed as part of our "collective unconscious." He suggested there were twelve archetypes that reflect our dominant personalities (for example Creator/Artist, Sage, Rebel, and Caregiver).[25] We are going to focus on a set of archetypes (and their shadow characteristics) that I have witnessed in myself and countless women around me. These are loosely based on other archetypes I've studied, but are mostly my own invention from years of working with women.

These archetypes take shape as a result of familial influences, social pressures, religious beliefs, and other outside forces. There are positives and negatives to each archetype, depending on how they play out in your life. It's important to identify which archetypes are impacting and possibly not serving you. When you can pinpoint these patterns, you can use them to your advantage or shift out of them so you can make more empowering choices.

Most people avoid doing this deep work because they want to stay comfortable and avoid pain. Confronting what holds us back can open up old wounds, and sometimes we trick ourselves into thinking we'll be better off if we stay where we are. Those wounds are controlling you, though; you've given your power to them and the only way to take your power back is to dive in, face them, and learn from them. Self-reflection is a gift: our past ordeals are often our greatest teachers. Doing this work will allow you to find peace. Confronting your archetypes and healing those wounds can help you overcome them. You'll be able to encourage others to work through their own trauma or negative behavior patterns too, and create a positive ripple effect. If you can't do it for yourself right now, do it for all of the other goddesses (or your children, partner, colleagues, loved ones) who will be inspired by you!

I know it can be daunting. I too have had to reprogram my patterns—over and over and over again. When I first went through this work I remember thinking, *There is no way I'm* that *archetype! Or that one!* But after some genuine, earnest soul searching, I realized I was. I had assumed so many roles, bounced around to different archetypes, and they were exhausting me emotionally. I was fatigued from playing out the same patterns day in and day out and recognizing them allowed me to grow and move past them (and now I can do this more quickly when certain archetypes rear their heads again).

You deserve to feel free, live joyfully, and move towards your wildest dreams. Be honest with yourself as you move through the archetypes and this work. Honor where you are. You may get uncomfortable or feel embarrassed. Forgive yourself. Please don't give up. You are strong and worthy, no matter which archetypes you identify with. You deserve to step into your power and live your best life as the very best archetype: goddess!

The Martyr

The Martyr is a woman who puts everyone before herself. Others' feelings, needs, and issues surpass her own. She is dedicated to making sure everyone else is thriving, but at a great cost to her personal happiness. She'll take the blame for others, even if she has nothing to do with the situation, because it makes her feel powerful. Her self-worth is derived from sacrificing for others, but she also resents never getting to be number one in her own life. She struggles to defend herself or speak up for her needs. The Martyr thinks this makes her selfless but in reality, it is selfish. She will eventually burn out from betraying herself over and over again, and wind up unable to help anyone. The Martyr believes she must suffer in order to be successful and equates self-worth with adversity, as well as how much she sacrifices for others.

Is this you?

It was definitely me. As a child of divorced parents, I carried a lot of baggage around abandonment. I clearly remember when I started feeling like I had to take care of everyone around me to make sure no one else worried about being left behind. I was five years old, and my parents had recently separated. Aya, who was three, and I were sitting on the couch with our dad. Both of us were leaning our heads against him, one on each side, staring blankly out the living room window. My sister, in her sweet little voice, whispered, "I miss Mom." Our dad started crying, then we started crying, and he said, "Me too." It was the first time I'd ever seen my father cry and it activated the Martyr in me. I knew, at five years old, that I had to protect my family at all costs.

The wound from my parents' split made me feel afraid I could be left behind at any moment (my parents never did anything to make me feel this way, but it's what manifested in me after their divorce). The antidote to that fear was to step into the role of the Martyr: to try to make everyone else feel heard, seen, understood, accepted, and safe.

Eventually this affected my relationships with my friends and peers too. People from school would open up to me about their tough home lives. Within weeks, I had somehow become my school's secret guidance counselor. I would provide a friendly ear and give advice to fellow students who were self-harming, depressed, suicidal, being abused at home, dealing with alcoholic parents, and many other horrible things. They'd show me their bruises and scars, and tell me about their pain. I couldn't understand it, but I absorbed every ounce of their suffering, their fears, and their sadness. I was only twelve, but I was already sacrificing my own mental wellbeing in order to be their therapist, life coach, and accountability partner.

I should have told them to seek professional help. I could have spoken to an authority figure at school. I didn't have to take all of that on, but it made me feel important—significant—to be able to give them the love and support I knew they weren't getting from their friends or family. Maybe I helped some of them, but it was to my own detriment. I started having anxiety attacks and couldn't function normally. When things didn't turn out okay for one of my friends or peers, I felt overwhelming guilt, as if I had somehow failed them. The Martyr programming was deeply programmed in me. It was the only way I knew how to cope, to feel influential.

As I entered adulthood, my friends continued to seek me out for advice and be uplifted (and the problems got more intense and complicated). I'd get stuck in a vicious cycle:

help my friends, feel amazing, and then devolve into feeling frustrated and drained. But then a friend would say, "When I'm with you, I feel better" or "I need to be around you more often," and then I would feel important and fulfilled all over again. They felt love and connection; I felt valued and respected. It was nice I could be a positive influence, but I was actually enabling instead of empowering them.

I struggled with this in my business as well. I had beautiful dreams and a big vision. I was really good at what I did. I had an amazing team with people whom I really cared about. They had so much aptitude and heart! I could see what they were capable of achieving. I cheered for them, supported them, counseled them, tried to motivate them . . . and waited and waited and waited for them to realize their potential. No matter how hard I tried to rally everyone, we weren't moving forward and I was afraid to leave them behind. What kind of leader, friend, *person* would I be if I didn't wait for them to figure out how awesome they were?! The Martyr in me felt trapped, obligated to stay by their sides, no matter how little they wanted to try. Part of me also believed that in order to make it to the top of my company I would have to endure hardship and pain in order to really "be worthy." Eventually, through lots of personal development, I realized that mentality wasn't serving me and I had to work my business for myself because I deserved success—even if no one wanted to follow me. And then, in a cruel twist, when my business *was* doing well, I worried my family would feel neglected. This was no way to lead a healthy, successful, independent life!

For fifteen years the Martyr archetype held me back from my greatness. Then I finally faced and overcame that wound and set boundaries that started to serve me.

No one, at any age, should feel responsible for anyone else's well-being and life (unless, of course, you are a parent of a little one). You don't have to be deliberately inattentive or mean, but the happiness of others is their responsibility, not yours. Helping others is a beautiful quality of the Martyr, but it rarely comes from a place of abundance and self-love; it usually comes from a place of codependency or the need to be liked. It isn't your job to save people from their misery. There are professionals who dedicate their lives to the sort of work that Martyrs take on; if you find yourself slipping into this archetype, it's important to give yourself permission to stop and refer whomever is leeching your time and energy to an appropriate and qualified resource. This will be better for you *and* them, I promise!

The Mother

If you are a mother with children, you may automatically assume this is your primary archetype. But that is not always the case! As you read through this section, see if you identify with the "shadow" qualities of the Mother. You may or may not, but know that even as a mom, the Mother archetype does not have to be your main behavioral pattern.

The Mother is similar to the Martyr, but with a little nuance. The Mother is a natural caretaker. She is nurturing, protective, caring, thoughtful, and empathetic—sometimes to a fault. The Mother is prone to coddling friends, loved ones, colleagues: she does work for others when they should do it themselves; she always "knows what's best;" she is overly accommodating to people who need to learn to think and act independently. Sometimes she is taken advantage of, while other times she is resented by those around her because she is too controlling. Like the Martyr, she often puts other people's needs ahead of her own and often winds up drained and exhausted, unable to fulfill her own desires. She is often in positions of leadership, but is susceptible to micromanagement.

Have you ever gone out with friends and because everyone else knew you would take care of them, they got belligerently wasted and you were forced to make sure they were safe? Were you always the one holding your girlfriend's hair back or making your roommate soup when they were sick? Or stopping your best friend from sending that regretful text? Or dispensing advice to everyone for all their problems? Are you someone who always worries about others' safety and wellbeing? If so, you might be the Mother.

You may feel amazing every time you do one of these things, but are you doing them out of a genuine desire to serve, or because it makes *you* feel good? And if it makes you feel good, how long does the feeling last? Do you typically wind up feeling spiritually empty? The Mother garners significance and love from helping and taking care of others, but in doing so she often denies herself peace and self-love, and those she helps miss out on the opportunity to grow.

The Mother, albeit usually subconsciously, takes pleasure in controlling those around her. If she continues to make others need her, she is always in control of the situation and can keep everyone safe in their comfort zones. This can lead to feeling abandoned or unloved if her "children" (whomever she has been taking care of) eventually grow up, move on, or find a new "mother."

Moms can fall into the Mother archetype because they wind up designing every facet of their lives around their children, instead of cultivating interesting and fulfilling lives for themselves. They're trapped in the need to be needed while continuously trying to pour from an empty cup. Conversely, sometimes those who did not feel they received enough love from their own mothers will become the Mother in order to project the love they wanted as children onto other people.

In addition to the Martyr, I myself have often identified as the Mother—even long before I had my daughter. I always wanted to be like my mom, who made my sister and me her whole world. She was so loving and caring, and I wanted to pass that on to others—to be a source of comfort to those in need. But I can also see now, after having done this deep work, that what I really wanted was to feel good like *she* did when we, her children, showed her affection. Her eyes would light up and she'd beam a huge smile any time Aya or I told her we loved her, gave her hugs, or made her little gifts. I craved that sort of attention and unconditional devotion too. So I took care of my friends; I made sure they were safe when they partied and was always the designated driver. But I would always feel so tired the next day; I was mentally, emotionally, and spiritually wiped out. My friends knew they could count on me, which felt good, but again—at what cost? I was unhealthy, sleep deprived, and, quite frankly, spending way too much money on gas!

After going through the same "Mother/Martyr" cycles for nearly two decades, I decided to break the pattern. It was scary to throw up boundaries with friends and business partners, but I knew it would show me where I needed to focus my time, energy, and love. I cut off or took a step back from friends who always took and never gave. I stopped "mothering" my teammates so they could learn how to fly on their own. I lost some friends, but the ones who remained supported me in my journey. And the best part was, this choice created space and allowed me to meet new people who didn't need "mothers," but wanted real, healthy friendship!

It's okay to want to be a nurturing goddess who looks after and supports others, but remember the "light" side of the Mother archetype is about filling your cup first. Allow others to grow and lift them up when they fall, but do not base your identity on needing to be needed. The *Dea* takes time for self-care and rest, and receives significance and self-worth from herself; she does not have to cater to everyone else's needs in order to be validated. She wants her children, friends, colleagues, and loved ones to evolve beyond needing her. She practices "tough love" when necessary, establishes personal boundaries, and says "no" when needed. She is like a lighthouse: a glowing beacon of guidance and safe support; but in order to nourish and serve others, she must be overflowing with light and positive energy. If her light goes out, she cannot assist anyone else.

The Prostitute

I know you might be saying, "Oh I am definitely *not* the Prostitute!" but don't bypass this section. Remember to be honest with yourself as you do this work. The Prostitute archetype does not have to be taken literally in terms of selling one's physical body for sex in exchange for money. The Prostitute archetype is about the pattern of "selling" your Divine energy or power, your mind, your beliefs or values, *or* your body for financial gain or security. The Prostitute could also be referred to as a "sell out;" abandoning a part of yourself for security within the human masculine world. She gives or trades her Divine light to others to feel secure. She also avoids conflict, exchanging her personal achievements or satisfaction for others' comfort or advancement. The

153

Prostitute usually manifests when a person has low self-esteem and hasn't yet awakened their inner goddess.

Have you ever stayed in a job you hated because it paid you well? Have you ever vouched for a product you didn't use or didn't like to make a quick buck? Perhaps you've campaigned for something or someone who did not align with your ethics or morals, but you wanted to gain resume experience? Or maybe you're staying in a relationship that is toxic, abusive, or stagnant because your partner provides you with a certain security or lifestyle? All of these are behaviors associated with the Prostitute.

Here is a more specific example. You decide you want to eat more nutritiously, eliminate junk food from your diet, and exercise consistently in the evenings after work. Your partner, however, has grown accustomed to you picking up fast food or takeout on your way home from work and spending the evening on the couch watching television. When you decide to change your habits, they get mad at you, which makes you feel threatened and insecure in your relationship. In order to "keep the peace" and maintain comfort in your relationship, you abandon your plans to eat well and get fit.

I found myself experiencing the Prostitute archetype when I was in my late teens/early twenties. After high school, my sister and I were able to live in our dad's house. He worked in another city and was rarely home, except for on weekends, so we basically had free reign (and free rent!). It may seem like that was a great deal, but what I realize now was it held me back from working towards what I truly desired. I was staying in my comfort zone and even convinced myself I'd feel guilty if I left because I'd be abandoning my sister and dad. My father was my benefactor and I took advantage of his generosity and parental kindness for much longer than I probably should have. Of course he loved supporting us and having us home all the time, but I relied too much, for too long, on this sense of financial and familial security, which in turn kept me from building my business in the way I wanted to deep down. My comfort kept me playing small and safe.

As with all archetypes, the Prostitute provides us with an opportunity to learn and grow; to understand our worth and potential. We don't need to sell out our minds, bodies, or souls to have the financial and physical security we desire. The goddess knows she is solid and secure, regardless of her current circumstances. She knows that when she stands strong in her Divine power, she can feel amazing on her own. Her soulful, confident energy will naturally attract abundance and the flow of money because she will be doing something that excites her! She can birth/create anything she wants.

The *Dea* knows she doesn't need anyone or anything outside of herself to support and take care of her. She knows the Universe always has her back. She stands in her truth and moves forward with her growth, ignoring anyone who tries to stop her. She makes plans to leave the job she hates by starting her own business. She values her ethics over experience. She no longer accepts money to promote a product or service in which she doesn't fully believe. If she is being abused or manipulated, she will get help or leave or make drastic changes to her boundaries and standards. And if her partner doesn't want to eat the healthy meals she makes, she tells him to make his own damn dinner.

The Basic

The Basic archetype is about so much more than pumpkin spiced lattes and Ugg boots. The Basic tries to be like everyone else and fit into societal norms in order to feel accepted. She values quantity of friends over quality and wants to be popular more than respected. She doesn't really know who she is and carries a false sense of confidence— "ego confidence" versus "soul confidence." Ego confidence comes from a place of thinking you are better than others, which usually is indicative of deep wounds of unworthiness. Soul confidence, however, comes from a place of knowing who you are, speaking your truth, and embracing your Divine power. It's understanding you can do and create anything simply by serving others and sharing your brilliant light.

The Basic struggles with soul confidence, and feels the need to overcompensate with material possessions and "elite" experiences (which she typically brags about on social media or amongst her friends) in order to feel worthy. She shows up in the world as a pretty, cute girl who seemingly wants to spread good vibes, but in reality— behind the scenes—she picks apart every aspect of herself. She prioritizes others' opinions and approval of her over her own self perceptions. She changes herself to be like the people she's around, desperate to be "cool." The Basic is lost and can't see her true beauty or power because she thinks they are extrinsic. Inside she feels empty; her life is a facade.

It can be hard to see if you're stuck in the Basic archetype but I urge you to closely examine your behaviors, your lifestyle, and the way you present yourself to the world. Do you hide or refrain from sharing your true opinion, perception, or feelings in order to be approved of by those around you? Do you allow the judgements of others to keep you from following your dreams? Do you keep toxic friends in your life because they get you into cool clubs but make you feel small and insecure all the time? Do you stay in your stagnant relationship because you want to be able to post photos of you and your boyfriend on social media so old high school classmates will think you're happily in love?

There have been many times I fell into the Basic archetype, particularly when I was younger and still finding myself. I would do whatever everyone else did, just to be accepted. At times, I'd play into the idea of only posting the "highlight reel" on social media, but would later realize my posts didn't accurately reflect who I was or how I was actually feeling on the inside. I was hiding in the spiritual closet, afraid to show my true beliefs because I was worried the people around me would think I was weird. There have been many times I've thought about enhancing my looks (*beyond* makeup) because I was seeing how normalized it was online. I've gotten hair and lash extensions, and mani-pedis, but now I try to evaluate why I want these things before I get them—because I want to have fun and pamper myself (the goddess), or because I think I'll be better/more likeable with them (the Basic)?

When I worked in the bar scene doing promotions for different venues, I completely lost sight of my true, powerful self. My nights were spent enticing people to party and then, for compensation, my coworkers and I would get bottles of hard liquor and VIP status. Drinking alcohol was not in my best interest and definitely disconnected me from anything Divine. I became like any other drunk girl in the bar or club, playing the Basic, desperate to fit in, have fun, and be cool. But the flashy lights of the vibrant nightlife scene caused me to dim my own special light. After months of participating in this toxic cycle, I felt completely depleted mentally and emotionally, and was more depressed than ever (even though I was supposedly having "so much fun" every weekend). I didn't love myself and was disrespecting my body by filling it with toxic drinks, eating unhealthy foods, and barely sleeping.

The Basic relies on external validation, which can often manifest as an addiction to shopping, changing her appearance, bragging on social media, etc. She is always filling her closet with the "hot new trendy" clothes, purses, and jewelry. She dyes her hair or gets a tattoo or piercing not because she really wants it (because there's nothing wrong with that!) but because she feels like she is "supposed to" in order to fit in. Sometimes the Basic shows up in relationships—staying with a partner when there is no depth or connection because your affiliation with that person makes you feel better about yourself (superficially, not soulfully). Some women and girls pride themselves on being "basic bitches," but they are so much more than that; they are unique, Divine goddesses waiting to be discovered.

When the *Dea* shows up, she helps the Basic begin the journey of profound introspection. She gently chaperones the Basic from the ego's crashing waves along the shore to the rich depths of the soul's ocean. The *Dea* knows she needs no one's approval. Her radiant beauty shines from deep within and requires no material additions. The *Dea* is proud of her perspective, her light, her differences, and her Divine individuality. She prefers a few close soul sisters, who love her for who she truly is, over thousands of fake friends or followers. The *Dea* will help you discover the beauty within you. She can connect you to whom you've always been, whom you are, and whom you will always be—not basic, but *extraordinary.*

The Victim archetype blames someone or something else for everything "wrong" in her life. Many times, the Victim *has* faced trauma or difficult circumstances, but instead of owning the pain and moving through it (remember forgive, heal, grow?), she falls into a pattern of blaming and victimhood. Victims say they need and desire help, but oftentimes they don't want to change because it would require effort and blaming others is "easier." Staying the Victim allows her to feel as though she's fulfilling many of her human needs: significance, certainty, love, connection, and even uncertainty. She focuses on all of the things that have gone wrong instead of on her blessings. She constantly shares her hardships with others (often Mother and Martyr archetypes!) because she gets love, connection, and attention from their sympathy and/or commiseration.

The Mother and Victim archetypes perpetuate each other's destructive patterns: the Mother is attached to saving the Victim and puts all her energy, love, and nurturing instincts into helping the Victim; the Victim gets all of the love, connection, and significance she needs from the Mother. The Victim will play out this cycle with new people throughout her whole life until she decides to heal and take responsibility for herself.

I often fell into the trap of playing the Victim as I grew my health and wellness business. I would think, *Why me? Why won't anyone join me? Why are people so judgmental? Why isn't my team working harder? I do so much, and I get nothing but drama and financial struggle in return!* I blamed my lack of success on my relatives who mocked me. I blamed my parents because I felt like they didn't believe in my big dreams. I blamed my teammates because I thought they weren't doing enough or working as hard as I was. What I eventually realized was, I didn't need anyone's approval to be prosperous in my business because I knew I was doing meaningful work. I didn't need my parents to believe in me because I believed in myself. And I didn't need my teammates to do the work—only I could be responsible for my success or blamed for my "failures."

In Jack Canfield's book, *The Success Principles™*, the *very* first principle is to take full responsibility for your life.[26] No more blaming others for what has happened. I know it's difficult, especially when other people have hurt you. And maybe it wasn't your fault, but spending all of your time centering yourself as the victim won't allow you to triumph beyond the adversity or pain. Ask yourself, "What can I learn from this situation?" and then . . . learn from it! Look at your hardships as opportunities for growth, not as setbacks. As spiritual teacher Dr. Wayne Dyer says, "When you change the way you look at things, the things you look at change."[27] Focus on solutions, not problems; from what has gone wrong, to what has gone right. Identify and celebrate the lessons that come from the challenges of life. Stop giving negative people or situations power. Forgive them and move on; bless and release. Then, and only then, will you stop being the Victim, own your power, and be truly free.

The *Dea* is a victor, not a victim. Reconnect to your own divinity and watch your life transform. Celebrate the miracle you are. This hard work must be done in the light, by focusing on gratitude, appreciation, and love (that does not mean darkness isn't a normal part of life, and a necessary balancing force, but we do not have to spend all of our time there and we certainly won't grow if we stay there). Life is happening *for* you, not *to* you, and your entire life will change when you shift your thoughts, beliefs, and daily actions to align with a more positive, less agonizing reality.

The Damsel in Distress

Most of us grew up watching movies or reading fairy tales in which the main character was a damsel in distress: Rapunzel in her tower, in need of rescue; Ariel under the sea, longing for life on land; or Snow White and Sleeping Beauty, both asleep and awaiting true love's kiss. For decades, *centuries*, young girls have been conditioned to believe they need a man to save them. And thus, the Damsel in Distress archetype (not to mention patriarchal, heteronormative standards for romance) has been deeply ingrained in the mindsets of girls and women.

The Damsel in Distress often overlaps with the Victim archetype, depending on the situation. She is not a woman who truly stands in her Divine power because she is always looking for a romantic partner to carry her (as opposed to walking in their own Divine power by her side). She will give her partner the world, but still feel empty. She puts her happiness, joy, worthiness, and life into her partner's hands. And if she doesn't have a partner, she spends all her time searching for one. The Damsel in Distress is constantly on the hunt for "Prince Charming," as opposed to cultivating self-love, and thinks finding the "perfect man" is the only way to feel happy and worthy. Instead of making a beautiful, independent life for herself, she waits around, hoping to be saved. Sadly, even when she finds a partner, she will rarely feel fulfilled because she hasn't spent any time learning how to be happy with herself as an individual. And more often than not, they won't live up to the unrealistic expectations she's seen depicted in rom-coms and story books.

After a few years of feeling trapped in toxic relationships—being lied to, cheated on, manipulated, and totally fooled—I took on the Damsel in Distress archetype. I started looking for a guy to fill the void left from broken relationships and to save me from past hurts and deceptions. Instead of turning inward, to deepen my relationship with my inner goddess, I looked for a guy to make me feel good. I desperately wanted to find my missing piece, my other half, the one who would "complete me." After searching and being let down time and time again, I finally realized I was the only one who could complete me. I cleared my field of all past partners and pain in order to move on and begin the deep inner work of awakening my *Dea*. This was the period of time during which I didn't date or have any intimate interaction with men. I wanted to be happy with myself, by myself. I was determined to be happily alone and to stop worrying about meeting the "man of my dreams." I set standards for love that aligned with the self-growth I was experiencing, knowing if I was meant to fall in love, it would only be with my twin flame.

The only person who can save you is you, dear goddess. When you work on filling yourself up to be whole on your own, you'll no longer feel like the Damsel in Distress, but the Divine *Dea*. And when you shine with Divine radiance and light, you will find you shine even brighter with the right partner, as opposed to having to dim your light for them.

SIDENOTE: Luckily, many more movies are being made about strong, independent female heroines who save themselves. Animated films like *Moana* and the *Frozen* franchise directly correlate to the rise of the Divine Feminine! *Moana* makes me cry every time. There is so much depth and heart: Moana is brave and determined to follow her Divine guidance in order to help her people; and then there is Te Fiti, the beautiful "Mother Earth" goddess who is on the hunt for her heart, which was stolen by a demi-god (a metaphor for human masculine greed, perhaps?). In both *Frozen* films, the main love story is between the sisters (which always brings me to tears because of how much I love my own sister). In *Frozen II*, Elsa goes on a magical journey to restore Divine balance in her land. She is called to a special, mythical place by a mysterious voice. She keeps asking the divine spirit to show herself, but what Elsa ultimately realizes is that she was the goddess all along (I'm not crying, you are!). I am so grateful my daughter gets to grow up watching and learning from these incredible stories about powerful women who are their own heroes.

The Shadow

The Shadow archetype lives beyond the light, obscured by others' prominence and power. She is uncomfortable celebrating her successes or wins, and downplays her greatness at every turn. She is self-deprecating and criticizes herself constantly. She is awkward when receiving praise or being acknowledged for a job well done. The Shadow craves validation from others, but also doesn't accept or feel comfortable with commendations; it's a vicious cycle of yearning for approval, but rejecting it when she finally receives it.

As the Shadow, she metaphorically hides in the shadows cast by those around her; though she is brilliant inside, she lacks the self-belief needed to shine. She has determined she's a sidekick, a co-star, a supporting character in other people's narratives—never the leading lady in her own story. The Shadow believes she operates better behind the scenes and steers clear of the spotlight—not because she is shy or introverted, but because she feels undeserving of attention. The root of the Shadow archetype is low self-esteem and unworthiness. Often these core limiting beliefs of the Shadow manifested at a young age, usually the result of bullying, unsupportive adults (parents, teachers, etc.), or sometimes even something relatively harmless that wound up hurting her more than she realized at the time.

The Shadow shows up in many ways. Have you ever not shared an idea at work because you were afraid your coworkers or boss wouldn't think it was good? Have you ever been in a relationship in which you let your partner make all the decisions, big or small—where to vacation, what to have for dinner, where to live, when to have kids, etc.? Have you ever felt like you didn't want to be successful in your business because you were worried you might outshine your best friend, sibling, or spouse? Have you ever been so concerned with things being "perfect" that you never actually started that art project, or book, or new business venture?

Perfectionism is actually a huge behavioral pattern of the Shadow archetype. As my friend Ashley said in a speech once, "Perfectionism is procrastination dressed up in a fancy costume." It's so true! Perfectionism leads to procrastination (and ultimately paralysis—being frozen with fear and self-doubt). Perfectionism is an illusion. It's an excuse not to put forth effort, a clever form of subconscious self-sabotage. The Shadow is convinced that even if she tried, her results would never be good or "perfect" enough, so why bother.

The Shadow is also negatively activated by others' success or confidence. She doesn't realize her triggers are indicators of places where she needs to heal, and generally have nothing to do with the other person. She's afraid she isn't as talented, as beautiful, as intelligent, or as creative as the goddesses around her, not realizing she too is a goddess, capable of being talented, beautiful, intelligent, and creative! She feels intimidated and compares herself to others; she mistakenly assumes their achievements are perfect and came without as much struggle as she has to endure (which can also be a symptom of the Victim archetype).

The Shadow definitely creeped in early on as I was establishing my business. I looked up to amazing women, who had created success and were living my dream life. I watched them onstage at our conference, inspired but also uncomfortable with the attention they were receiving. I thought, *I don't need to be up there. I'll just do my thing. I don't want the spotlight.* Of course, I didn't *need* the spotlight to be proud of my achievements or to be successful, but my desire not to have my hard work publicly recognized was actually the result of me playing it safe; playing it small. If others couldn't see how well I was doing, then they also wouldn't be able to see if I failed. I didn't want to be a star because I was afraid it could burn out or worse, other people would judge me or think I'd gotten too big for my proverbial britches. I was neglecting so much power and potential within me. I was ignoring my goddess, keeping her trapped and small, in the shadows. Eventually I had to realize I wasn't serving anyone by not allowing my story, struggles *and* successes, to be a source of encouragement for others. I knew I had to stop being self-conscious because if I was judging myself for wanting to be up on that stage, then I was judging all of the other phenomenal goddesses who were thriving—and I knew I didn't want to do that!

You'll know you've moved beyond the Shadow archetype when you're able to spend your time improving yourself, feeling totally self-validated and proud of your hard work, and finally feeling worthy of success. When people ask how you're doing, instead of downplaying your happiness, career achievements, or healthy relationship, you'll be able to say, "I'm fantastic!" or "Things are going great!" or "I am healthy and happy and crushing it at the office!" You'll stop comparing yourself to others and be thrilled for them when they are achieving their dreams.

The lesson the Shadow provides is this: stop comparing yourself to others and step into your power—bravely, confidently, and unapologetically. If there are people in your life whom you feel are holding you back or keeping you down, have those tough conversations. Talk to your partner so you can be on the same page and build each other up. Speak with your family and stand firm in your resolve to follow your dreams; tell them you want their support, but don't *need* it.

Your *Dea* wants you to be center stage! You are the star of your own life, so stop lurking in the shadows and let your light shine! You are worthy of everything you desire. Confidence and success will not magically show up until you put in the work and can be proud of it. The more you practice, the better you'll get, so stop worrying about being perfect and get to work! Your gifts, your calling, are much better "imperfectly" completed and out serving the world than never started or left unfinished. Perfection is unachievable and boring, anyway! We are all divinely imperfect and unique, so honor the *Dea* by reminding yourself that you are capable of anything. Stop playing small, start having fun, and shine bright, goddess!

Breaking the Mold

When negative shadow patterns are deeply ingrained, it can feel like you are dragging your feet through life with weighted chains around your ankles. To break the mold of these archetypes, you must set boundaries—healthy, loving boundaries—with everyone in your life. This will establish a barrier that will protect your energy and power, and help prevent you from falling into a negative spiral of draining your life source or dimming your light for others. In setting these boundaries, you will also give others the opportunity to break their own toxic cycles.

Remember: when you set boundaries with people who are not ready to grow themselves, you may be met with resistance, guilt trips, and sometimes even anger. People who are trapped in their own archetypes won't want you to grow past them and will feel threatened by your newfound self-confidence and success. Do not be thrown off course— the Universe is giving you another opportunity to evolve to a higher state and further awaken your Dea

Release the shadow aspects of the archetypes that aren't serving you. Stop allowing the same conversations to occur over and over again. Spend more time working on yourself instead of trying to solve other people's problems. Be the example for others to change themselves. Give the people in your life the opportunity to learn their own lessons without giving them all the answers. Stop trying to save others. Release your attachment to others' lives and set yourself free to live in alignment with your Dea.

Create space for new patterns that are supportive to your dreams and growth. This may sometimes involve changing your environment and/or the people surrounding you. You have to proactively choose not to participate in your old patterns and dynamics. If you catch yourself slipping back into one (or several!), be kind and forgive yourself. Then, find a way to pull yourself out with conscious awareness. For example: if you've identified you're the Basic archetype, you might be prone to gossiping, perhaps in order to leverage popularity with a certain group of friends. Now that you have identified your archetype and decided to stop gossiping, you may have to stop hanging out with friends who enable it. Or change/remove yourself from the conversation when people start bad mouthing someone who isn't present. If it's really insidious, be brave and tell them to stop (this will usually serve as a wakeup call for the gossip mongers too!).

If you are playing out a shadow archetype, sit down and write out all of the toxic patterns and cycles you want to release, and then all of the new beliefs and habits you want to create to replace them. You can even write them out as affirmations and add them to your "I AM" statements. Say them every day to start reprogramming your subconscious mind, which will in turn help you modify your thoughts, beliefs, and actions.

Chapter 14

True Transformation

"Yesterday I was clever, so I wanted to change the world. Today I am wise, so I am changing myself." - *Rumi* (Poet)

Many people don't know what they believe in and are lost spiritually. As I described at the beginning of the book, I felt disconnected from a greater power, which made me feel limited by my humanness. I tried to find God outside of myself, but couldn't. I tried to tap into some kind of Magic, but most things felt whimsical—flights of fancy, nothing grounded in a spirituality that felt authentic to me. When we are spiritually separated from our Divine power, we are like a thirsty traveler stumbling through the desert. We feel lost, stressed, unfulfilled, and may even suffer from depression and/or anxiety. Deep down we know there must be more to life, but we don't have the energy or direction to discover it. We're trapped in survival mode, doing our best to "get by," which leaves us feeling empty inside. We fill the void and numb ourselves with drugs, alcohol, prescription pills, TV, social media, high-risk sex, and other destructive behaviors.

We don't realize how much power we actually have over our lives. We think we're victims of our circumstances, that if we could only change our outer conditions, we could change our inner state of being. We become addicted to our emotions, doing whatever we can to feel the figurative (and sometimes literal) "high" of life. The thing is, we have the power to change our thoughts and choose to feel differently. I know it's hard to see when you're stuck in trauma or a negative situation, but our brains are incredible and oh-so-powerful.

In order to actually make a lasting change, we have to go deeper and understand how we operate as human beings. For the last few years, I have studied the work of Dr. Joe Dispenza and it is absolutely brilliant. He connects the missing pieces between science and spirituality. His discoveries are groundbreaking—I highly recommend digging into his books and teachings, but I want to share some highlights, as well as my interpretations, with you here.

According to Dispenza's work, we release over 1,300 chemicals into our bodies when we feel emotions like fear, depression, anxiety, or doubt. Our bodies create and release a cocktail of hormones and chemicals that hit the brain and put us into a state of fight or flight, which is ingrained in us to help us stay alive. In modern times, we rarely need this particular brand of "survival mode" because we aren't typically fleeing imminent danger, but our bodies haven't evolved that far yet. We are living unconsciously, subject to our most basic animal instincts, forgetting we are equipped with emotional intelligence and the power of choice![28]

Once you're aware you've been living life unconsciously, you can decide to transform. This won't happen overnight, of course. If your brain and body have been conditioned to feel fear, doubt, depression, or anxiety, they will continue to do anything to keep you in a state of familiar "comfort," otherwise known as your habits. Your body has been running on default programming for a long time, addicted to the particular chemical concoction it's been used to receiving. You have to be willing to consciously shift your thoughts, feelings, and actions every day. You may do well for awhile, but slip back into an old negative pattern. Keep going. This isn't about perfection (nor is it about denying true emotional or chemical imbalances some people face. Please seek medical attention in those cases and know there is no shame in getting therapy or taking medications if that is what you and your doctors have determined is the best course of action for you).

Your actions will match what you believe about yourself. Whatever you want to change or create in your life must become part of your identity, and then you must create a habit that mirrors what you believe about yourself. Some beliefs will only require a quick flip of a switch, while others may require hard work and consistent action, day in and day out. When you feel lost or unsure, connect with your *Dea* and ask her for guidance; imagine what she would do in order to get to that next major breakthrough

One of the biggest, most damaging negative patterns I had to overcome was in my business. For years, I would scrape by with minimal and/or last-minute effort (a cycle I'd perfected as a kid in school: wait till the last minute, cram for a test or scramble to finish a project, and then somehow still ace my work). Unfortunately, this pattern did not work for me as an adult. It was in no way a sustainable method of operation for a successful business! On the first day of every month I'd set a big goal, barely work for four weeks, and then desperately hustle on the last day or two. I'd be stressed and frantic, worried I wouldn't hit my goal (and no surprise, I rarely did). I expected the Universe to help me achieve massive goals, like a 400% increase in sales volume, but did I do four times as much work or serve four times as many people? No! My dreams were big, my expectations bigger, and yet I was caught in a pattern of limited belief and meager effort.

This behavioral pattern created an emotional cycle within me, something I refer to as the "drama pattern." I'd go from high energy and excitement to low vibe lethargy to disappointment and self-pity . . . which then turned into *extremely* negative self-talk. I'd enter a shame spiral and "should" all over myself: "I *should* have done this; I *should* have done that; I *should* have done more; I *should* have been better." The higher I'd set my goals, the lower and harder I'd fall when I didn't hit them. Instead of setting more realistic, incremental goals or changing my attitude and working harder, I lowered my standards, which then made me feel embarrassed, like I wasn't good at what I was doing (even though I knew deep down I was!). It went on like this for seven long, agonizing years.

Finally, I decided it was time to make a change. I was ready for the hard, deep work I knew would be required to awaken my *Dea* so we could co-create magic and success together. I was ready to confront and be honest with myself about my excuses and fears. I had to intentionally reprogram my tendencies and consciously choose to do something positive, every day, that would help me get closer to my goals.

This required a major shift in my identity. I wrote out a list of inspiring characteristics and beliefs I wanted to embody. I decided I was not only going to be a big dreamer, but a hard worker—someone who would get her work done, even when she didn't feel like it. Tasks that used to take me hours or days would be accomplished quickly and efficiently. I no longer made "to do lists" and instead scheduled my *priorities*. I was going to be self-disciplined, develop new habits without worrying about being perfect, read and watch positive books and training, and speak life over myself. My new identity meant I was a leader through action, not words. I was on a mission and had a vision to serve millions of people. Every minute, hour, and day I had to choose to identify as this new "Sammi 2.0." This is what true transformation can look like, if you allow it.

With this new identity, things changed quickly. I went from doing eight to ten business meetings a month to eight to ten *a day*. My soul felt on fire! I was inspired by every conversation and felt like I was finally doing the *work* required for the big dreams I had. I wasn't stressed anymore, but exhilarated—and, when I wasn't working, I could actually spend more quality time with my family because I wasn't distracted by all of the things I thought I *should* have been doing.

I went through a similar process when I decided to reshape my behavior patterns concerning my personal life. I had gotten into the habit of making long to-do lists, getting completely burnt out and overwhelmed by the long to-do lists, and then accomplishing absolutely nothing. I decided I no longer wanted this to be part of my identity, so I consciously adopted a new habit: doing things right away as I thought about them, especially if they wouldn't take more than a few minutes.

Unless you take conscious control, you'll be stuck in a cycle for weeks, months, even years, like I was. This will require you to use the power of your mind to take the driver's seat back from your body, which can go on autopilot otherwise. You'll have to become aware of the moments when you have quick reactions that are not in alignment with your new mindset. Sometimes you'll be triggered by a physical response: a pit in your stomach or a wave of nervous energy. When this happens, your body wants to revert to its old habits in order to stay safe and comfortable, but if you're aware of it, you can shift out of it more quickly.[29] The key is to slow the reaction down before it completely takes over. Close your eyes, take deep breaths, and relax your muscles (start at your feet and work your way up). Slowly roll your shoulders backwards until they loosen. And remind yourself who you are, what you want, and where you are. You may even have to do this aloud! You can say, "Hey, body! I honor what you're feeling but we're okay! We are safe. I am in control." This will allow you to pause, reassess what cycle you're stuck in, and allow the *Dea* to step in and work with you. Imagine retraining your mind and body to be addicted to feeling amazing, healthy, vibrant, connected, grateful, and joyful!

One of the best tools I can suggest for true transformation is meditation. Meditation is so powerful, and I promise it does not have to be done in any sort of "perfect" way. In fact, there are many different types of meditation, so I encourage you to have fun exploring which serves you best. There is guided meditation (Dispenza has some powerful ones on his website for purchase[30]), silent meditation, visualization meditation, Transcendental meditation, mantra meditation, moving meditation (like through yoga) . . . the list goes on and on! To me, meditation is simply focused time to be with yourself and connect inwardly. It is a time to silence the mind so you can allow your higher self in and/or receive guidance from your god or goddess, angels, spirit guides, etc. It allows you to slow down. Meditation can last thirty seconds or ten minutes or five hours—there is no minimum requirement *or* limit to how long you can enjoy or benefit from it. That being said, author Dr. Sukhraj Dhillon says, "You should sit in meditation for twenty minutes every day, unless you are too busy—then you should sit for an hour." Take time to meditate every day and watch your life change before your very eyes.

When you master the mind-body-spirit connection, you will realize that even when nothing seems to be happening, *everything* is happening. Meditation gives your "thinking brain" a break, which can allow limitless guidance, energy, and magic to flow. It can transform your life so you feel less stressed and chaotic, and more focused, productive, and in tune with the Divine's high, happy, loving vibration.

As I write this, people of the world are quarantined in their homes because of the COVID-19 pandemic. It is undoubtedly a terrifying time, and everyone seems to be handling it in different ways. I remember when things started getting more serious here in the United States and the real fear set in for me. It was a Friday afternoon and I was sitting in an empty juice bar, listening to updates from the President on my phone. People had been buying out the stores, depleting food and toilet paper supplies. Everyone was panicked. That night, my daughter came home from her first week of preschool with a fever and for the next three days, I was a total worried mess (it was just a cold, thank goodness). I was scared for her, for my family and friends, and for the world at large. Anxious thoughts repeated over and over again and I started to feel like all of the personal development and self-growth I had done over the years disappeared. On Monday morning, I woke up still worried but conscious that I needed to shift my energy before negativity and fear consumed me. I reflected back on the periods when I experienced my truest transformations and applied the tools and techniques I'd learned: I did some yoga; I went for a walk outside in the sun; I danced and shook my arms all over the place; and then I sat in a warm bath, closed my eyes, and opened myself up so my *Dea* could guide me.

Swoosh!

In an instant, after I'd slowed my breathing and calmed my mind, she appeared and I finally felt harmonious, peaceful, and filled with pure love again. I started to cry. Tears rolled down my face as I heard her say, "I love you and I am here for you all the way. No matter what you are feeling or learning, I am waiting for you to surrender and connect." I felt open again; each pore was venting every last bit of emotional tension I'd been carrying with me. The pain I'd been feeling acted as a catalyst for me to reconnect with my inner goddess, because I allowed it to. Since then, I've been able to show gratitude for this time of stillness and reflection. I've been working on this book, painting, spending quality time with my husband and daughter, taking regular walks in nature, and so much more.

Goddess, I want you to wake up and honor your inner power and potential. Light and love are available to you at all times, but you have to allow them in. Imagine what life can be! You'll have to go deeper than most others are willing, but it will be so worth it. Your true transformation may seem out of reach right now, depending on where you are in life, but you are on the right path and your unique journey is exactly as it should be. If you don't like where you are currently, be grateful because . . . it is showing you exactly what you no longer want! This darkness will help you find your light. Pain can lead to pleasure and peace, if you are willing to learn and truly transform from it.

SOUL WORK

Schedule time every day to sit (or lie down), without distractions, and meditate. Set the intention to connect with your *Dea* and allow her guidance to unfold. You can light a candle or use crystals, if you're called to do so, but remember there is no "right" or "perfect" method for meditation—just find what best aligns with you and your transformation goals.

If you can get to a place of true openness, you may feel vibrational energy moving through you. For me, it starts at the top of my head and moves down my spine, and then my arms and legs. This energy is my goddess, and when I feel her, I ask questions and for guidance, as well as show her appreciation for her love. The more I practice meditation, the longer I can hold that intense energy in my body.

I challenge you to meditate for thirty days straight, no matter what type of meditation or for how long you sit, and see what happens!

You can find guided meditations at AwakenDea.com or through a variety of apps on your phone.

Share your experience online with #IdeaSoulWork.

177

Chapter 15

Allowing Abundance

The average financial experience for most millennials these days feels anything but abundant. Rent is more expensive than what most young adults are able to make in a month, and home ownership seems completely out of the question. The average American is dependent on loans and credit cards, racking up thousands to tens and hundreds of thousands of dollars of debt. Millennials typically need several streams of income (we've been nicknamed the "gig generation") just to cover normal living expenses, and few can imagine ever having a robust savings account, or any savings at all. Most people around my age have to work several jobs and/or side hustles to make ends meet, with no benefits or long-term sustainability. All of this has added up to financial disaster, with little hope for improvement as far as "traditional" earnings and lifestyles are concerned.

But there's a bright side! Maturing and entering the workforce during this financial fiasco has forced millennials to get creative and think outside of the box. Entrepreneurship is on the rise as more and more of us seek to be self-employed and create financial opportunities for ourselves. Within this twisted economy, we have somehow managed to mine new opportunities, paving the way for future generations. Global connection, social media, and new technology have helped Gen-Y/Millennials/Gen-Z turn passions into paychecks, curiosity into cash, and fresh new ways of thinking into financial abundance.

I used to have many mental, emotional, and spiritual blockages when it came to money. Like many people, I believed that in order to be spiritually enlightened, I couldn't have a lot of money or material things. Or, in order to be successful and wealthy, I couldn't necessarily abide by my moral and ethical beliefs. Too often, when doing deep soul work, we mistake money and abundance for greed and selfishness. Of course there are people in this world who use money in misaligned or malicious ways. There are selfish, nasty, greedy people in the world and there are happy, generous, kind people in the world; the thing is, they can be rich *or* poor. Money amplifies the qualities that already exist within you—it doesn't *define* you.

The pursuit of gratuitous wealth has generated so much strife and negativity in this world. Natural resources are depleted. Entire groups of people are unjustly harmed and disenfranchised by unfair political and/or social systems, which have been designed by the very wealthy elite to keep everyone else impoverished and fighting over "table scraps." But it doesn't have to be that way.

Money and/or material possessions cannot make you happy alone, but by connecting with your inner goddess and welcoming abundance to flow to you, you can find *more* happiness, and certainly more ease and freedom from hardship in this complicated world. It is certainly harder to be broke than to be wealthy. We are all children of the Divine and deserve to live abundant lives, rich in experiences, love, peace, fun, and comfort—which looks different for everyone! Money is a tool, like a hammer, and can be used to build many different things. There are goddesses who are radiantly joyful living in a camper in the wilderness with very few things burdening them down. There are goddesses who travel the world in luxury and enjoy experiencing different cultures. And there are goddesses who want an idyllic home with a giant kitchen and their kids in private school. You do you, Sister.

You will create space for the big, beautiful vision you have for your life by removing any resistance you have around financial abundance. Until you identify what's holding you back when it comes to money, you are unlikely to attract more of it with any kind of ease or flow. This will require you to dig deeply into your old beliefs, and probably ancestral patterns, around money. Perhaps when you were young, your parents always said, "Money doesn't grow on trees" or "We're not made of money." Or you had a grandparent who complained about the "tax man" taking all of their money. Or noticed your family always used credit cards. Or you had a teacher who once said, "Money is the root of all evil." Dig in and see if you can identify where your gut reactions to money—both in terms of spending *and* receiving—come from. You may be shocked by how much your subconscious attitudes around money have been holding you back.

Money is a source of energy, its own entity (like a person) and you have a relationship with it, whether you realize it or not. Take a moment and reflect on your relationship with money as if you were evaluating a romantic partnership or marriage. How is it going? Is there respect, love, trust, and honesty? Or is it troubled, unreliable, angry, and depressed?

When I sat down and took a long, hard look at my relationship with money, I realized it was inconsistent, erratic, and horribly damaged. We were on again-off again, hot and cold, good and then bad. I'd tell money, "I like you! I want more of you!" and then, "Whatever, I don't need you, I'm happier without you." But then I'd say, "Wait! Come back!

I didn't mean it! I need you!" followed by, "You're evil and bad for me! I don't want anything to do with you!" Of course, I always circled back to, "I love you! Please forgive me! I didn't mean it, please don't leave me again!" Sounds like a pretty toxic relationship, right?! We would never tell our friends to stay with a partner who made them feel this way, which is exactly why money/abundance doesn't stick around for long when you treat it like this. Stop sending mixed signals to money and your relationship will be so much stronger. Money is attracted to those who consistently love it and use it for good.

It's no coincidence that a negative relationship with money can also lead to negativity in your interpersonal relationships. One of the top causes of divorce is miscommunication around finances and money, much of which is caused by differences between the Divine Feminine (flow) and human masculine (force). Because patriarchal culture has sought to suppress the Divine Feminine in order to amass power, money dynamics within relationships often become tainted and muddied. In a "traditional," heteronormative partnership/family, the man typically controls the money, while the woman must ask for funds or is given an allowance. This male-dominated hierarchy has created an imbalance throughout the decades (centuries). Ironically, the human masculine's need to control and limit the outflow of money leads to a lack of abundance.

Feminine energy/power is all about abundance of the Divine—the manifestation of everything we need to take care of ourselves and others. When a woman's ability to control finances is restricted, she will not be able to utilize her creative, Divine essence to manifest more abundance for the household. There should always be a healthy financial respect and communication around money within a partnership. Not every couple will handle their finances in the same way, and that's perfectly alright, but if you are not on the same page and can't talk openly and equally about money, things can end disastrously.

Reprogramming your money mindset is so necessary, not only in terms of negative patterns but also what you think is possible! What you think is a lot of money now may one day seem like a tiny amount. For instance, a few years ago, I thought making $5,000 a month was practically inconceivable. I *wanted* to make $5,000 every month, and knew other people were doing it, so it was technically attainable. I *thought* I believed I could make that much, but my belief was actually very shaky because I'd never seen it happen for me before. I had to up level my faith, as well as my self-confidence, work ethic, and feelings of worthiness. As I sharpened my mindset, dove into personal development, and got into more business activity (with a focus on *serving others* and adding more value, not just on acquiring more money), I ended up surpassing my monthly goal of $5,000 and proceeded to double, triple, and quadruple that in single months! What I learned was, if you want the money in your account to grow, *you* have to grow.

I also had a habit of spending whatever amount of money I made. I would convince myself I needed to spend money on the things I wanted so I could feel abundant and manifest more. Yes, you should feel abundant when spending money, but this pattern was actually coming from a place of lack and fear. I always seemed to take my bank account back to zero—even if I didn't need to spend the money! It was exciting to have more money than I'd ever had before, but the amount of money available to me hadn't changed my money habits. Once I became more aware of this issue, I was able to do some work around it. I realized my Divine

Feminine and Divine Masculine energies were out of balance!

Retail therapy is good every once and awhile, but I needed to be more aware of when and why I was shopping/spending my money. Was I doing it because I was feeling low-vibe and needed the adrenaline boost of something new, or was I doing it because the purchase genuinely made me feel happy? And once I had spent the money, did I feel grateful or resentful? When you can feel good about spending money, you'll attract more. Think of it as an energetic exchange, bartering for good vibes; otherwise, you'll be coming from a lack mindset. The *Dea* appreciates the ebb and flow of money. Say "Thank you!" any time you receive *or* spend money (after all, you couldn't spend it if you hadn't received it!). Create positive affirmations for your relationship with money, like "THERE'S MORE WHERE THAT CAME FROM!" "MONEY FLOWS EASILY AND FREQUENTLY TO ME!" "I AM A MONEY MAGNET!" "I AM ABUNDANT AND ATTRACTING MORE OF WHAT I LOVE!"

It is crucial that you learn how to feel good about spending money, even on things you typically think of as "negative," like bills or taxes. When you pay your bills, feel gratitude deep within for the services you have received—for everyone and everything that helped bring electricity into your home, clean water out of your faucet, food on your table, and a roof over your head. Many people don't have these luxuries and yet too many of us take them for granted every day.

I started applying more Divine Masculine qualities, like reason and strategy, to my financial planning and when I made purchases. One of my favorite money strategies has been to create different savings accounts for different things that are important to me and my family, such as travel, emergencies, a house, our children's education, taxes (particularly important for those of us who are self-employed/small business owners!), etc. Each month we put different percentages into each account. This works well for us; do some research to discover a system that works well for you and your family.

Breaking these patterns was essential to my personal growth and transformation into an abundant goddess. Through this work I realized I'd been conditioned to think there was only so much money to go around—duped into believing it was somehow finite. This prevented me from living with an abundant mindset and cultivating a positive relationship with money. The thing is, the natural Divine Feminine state of the earth is abundance!

Once, when we were driving through Gilbert, Arizona, I noticed an orchard lined with rows of beautiful, flourishing orange trees. The trees were overwhelmed with fruit, more than any one person could ever pick before they would eventually rot. It struck me as a beautiful metaphor for the abundance of this world—there is more than enough to go around, if we nurture it and allow it to grow. Eventually, when we are healthy and committed to growth, we will overflow with resources and be able to share with others. When you walk on the beach, you walk upon innumerable grains of sand, which extend far beneath the waves, across the entire ocean floor, to other continents. When you drive past a forest, you see thousands of trees as far as the eye can see, oxygenating our air, providing habitats to creatures great and small, and spreading seeds for more trees to grow. You are created from the same Divine perfection as every river, ocean, flower, and tree—why should you not also live in a state of constant and unquestionable abundance?!

Actual currency is manufactured every day, and most "money" these days exists purely as numbers on a screen— we so rarely actually touch physical cash or coins anymore. So why do we think of it as a depletable resource? Why do we make such a big deal out of safeguarding, stockpiling, and spending it? I invite you to stop feeling obsessed with and controlled by pieces of paper and start imagining money as a limitless, high-vibe energy source. Think of money as you would health. Feeling well and being in good health doesn't mean everyone else is sick—everyone can be healthy because good health is a limitless resource. In fact, when you prioritize being in good health, it can often inspire others to take better care of themselves. The more physical energy you have (not to mention the longer you live), the more you can create and make a difference in the world. The same goes for money: when you are in a state of financial abundance, you can create more and make more of a difference in the world.

The world needs goddesses and light-workers, who are pure of heart and generous in spirit *and* money, to step up, create abundance, and fuel positive change. We need to be intentional with the way we receive and exchange money; to serve others with our gifts and passions, and be compensated with positive energy (and yes, money!) in return. Honor your value. Be strong and firm when it comes to your worth, your time, your energy, and your money.

The *Dea* wants to show up BIG. She will expect you to step outside of your comfort zone, take risks, be bold, and follow your heart and intuition. The *Dea* is a money magnet because she shines her light brightly and serves others any and every way she can. Goddess, *you* are a money magnet. Expect abundance and watch it flow into your life, your wallet, and your bank account. You *deserve* money because you are generous, wise, and open-hearted with it. When money is in your hands, it will return to the world with more positive and enlightened energy because of how much you honor, respect, and appreciate it.

SOUL WORK

What are your BIG dreams?

Imagine making ten times the income you currently make. What is that number? If this is difficult for you based on your current mindset or financial reality, start by visualizing $10,000 a month flowing into your bank account. What would that look like? How would that change your life?

Take a few moments to write out every detail of your "10X" life. What would you do differently? Would you be at the same job/in the same career? Could you scale back your hours or retire? Would you have more time to volunteer? If so, who would you help? How would you give back? Would you start a business or non-profit? How much could you donate to your favorite charitable organization each month? Where would you live? What would your home look like? What kind of car would you drive? Would you travel? If so, where? Would you fly first class? Take a family cruise? In what kinds of hotels would you stay? How would you treat your friends and family? Take them on dream vacations? Buy them new cars? Pay off their student loans? Could you sponsor, adopt, or foster a child or an animal? Would you pay off debt? Would you pamper yourself and those you love more?

When you have a clear vision, and apply the heart and work required, this does not have to be a dream life—it can *BE* your life!

Share your experience online with #IdeaSoulWork.

Chapter 16

The New Age of Business

There is a sexist, human masculine belief that women are unfit to run major corporations or hold political office because of "wild mood swings" and a tendency to be "hyper emotional." Even in 2020, with a *record number* of female CEOs, only 37 Fortune 500 companies are run by women.[31] In the United States House of Representatives and Senate, women make up only 23% and 25% respectively, in spite of making up over half the population.[32] The world is in dire need of equal representation and some serious Divine Feminine magic. When we challenge businesses to incorporate more of the Divine Feminine into their practices, like balancing profits *with* people (worker welfare, fair trade, safe ingredients, etc.) and the planet (sustainable harvesting, clean energy, biodegradable ingredients, compostable/recyclable packaging, etc.), the world will undoubtedly feel more balanced, peaceful, and happy.

In the 1910s, Henry Ford wanted to take his company's profits and distribute them to employees instead of giving it all to shareholders. Some shareholders, including the Dodge brothers, didn't like that—they wanted to use their shares to start their own car companies.[33] The Dodge brothers sued Ford, which initiated our modern corporate structure. This imbalanced business model is designed to keep money in the hands of the few, while simultaneously failing to fairly compensate workers for their hard work or ensure the production of safe, high-quality, affordable products and services. Most people can't afford luxury

189

products or services on their minimal pay. In fact, in 2017, a study by CareerBuilder showed that 78% of workers were living paycheck to paycheck.[34] These elitist, exclusionary business practices cannot continue.

The New Age of Business is all about "compassionate capitalism," with a focus on serving and helping and not profiteering. Imagine if the hierarchy of organizations wasn't as important as the heart of what they were producing/the services they were providing. What if every single person was seen as a crucial team player in a company, and not just faceless, nameless cogs of a massive corporate machine? To me, compassionate capitalism is about treating employees fairly, prioritizing their wellbeing and health over the bottom line. It's about listening to everyone's ideas, meeting all employees' needs, and creating a supportive, nurturing work environment. People should feel like their managers, bosses, and/or CEOs have their backs and appreciate them. If employees felt valued at work, they would feel more loyal and professionally fulfilled. Compassionate capitalism is also about lowering expenses and making safe, healthy products available to everyone.

Moral and ethical business practices, integrity, heart-centered leadership are at the heart of compassionate capitalism, which I believe is the wave of the future. And women belong at the forefront.

Too many women deprive themselves of the opportunity to thrive in the business world, however, for a multitude of reasons, both external and internal. For the sake of awakening the inner goddess, let's focus on the latter. This internal hesitation to pursue business endeavors is the result of a "fixed mindset," as described by Stanford professor and psychologist Carol Dweck.[35] Those with a fixed mindset believe they are incapable of change because they "are who they are." They avoid challenges due to a fear of failure, and believe they are not as intelligent, talented, or worthy of success as other people.

Many of us are programmed at a young age to believe our productivity or quantifiable achievements determines our worthiness. If we got good grades or scored the winning goal, we were celebrated by our teachers, parents, and coaches; if we got poor marks, we most likely got punished or critiqued in some way. Most of us were put into some category or box, based on arbitrary measures of intelligence, talent, athletic ability, creativity, etc. We weren't given the space to grow or learn in our own unique ways, and compared ourselves to and competed with our peers, siblings, and teammates. As we grew up, we sought approval from our professors, employers, and mentors, and found ourselves competing with our coworkers, friends, and sometimes even our romantic partners. We're trapped in a cycle of "do, do, do," afraid if we stop achieving, we aren't worthy of approval or worse, someone might outperform us. This leaves us spiritually drained and mentally exhausted with no capacity for growth—which is no way to run an aligned business.

Having a fixed mindset will keep you stagnant in your life; a self-fulfilling prophecy of lethargy and mediocrity. Success in business, or life in general, requires a "growth mindset." Those with a growth mindset believe they are capable of anything! They embrace obstacles and see challenges as opportunities to evolve and get better. They crave knowledge, and develop their intelligence, creativity, and talents through constant training and personal development. Transformation is *so much easier* when you embrace a growth mindset. See your life as a series of educational experiences, and not as successes or failures. Making this switch can be difficult at first, but can get easier by celebrating every victory, and making sure you praise others for their attempts, persistence, creativity, etc. as opposed to feeling competitive or jealous. It is important not to wait for others to celebrate or approve of you. This will help create a positive environment for future growth, generate confidence, foster a resilient spirit, and make yourself and those around you feel good!

Having a growth mindset is a choice. You can see things as obstacles and make excuses to quit, or you can see roadblocks as opportunities to innovate and develop your skills. The best example of this comes from children. When babies are trying to take their first steps, they stumble and fall constantly. Do they give up and crawl forever? Of course not! Babies are naturally equipped with a growth mindset, undeterred by external forces. In fact, everyone around them cheers and claps whether they successfully walk or not because they want to encourage them to keep going—so why don't we do this for ourselves?! As my dad used to say, "Practice. Practice. Practice."

I've learned so much about having a growth mindset from my two-year-old daughter. Recently, she was playing in her little toy kitchen. She started yelling and crying in frustration because she couldn't get her play phone to hook on the side of her fridge. She'd try to hang it up quickly, it would fall off, and she'd cry out in exasperation. I gently said, "You can do it baby. Try very gently to place the phone." She tried again, it fell again, and she was clearly still very discouraged. I encouraged her more. "You can do it! Gentle, gentle." She tried again, and this time, it stayed! My husband and I clapped and cheered for her, at which point her furrowed, frustrated brow softened and her sweet face beamed with a confident smile. She demonstrated her potential to keep trying, make progress, and learn something new—even though it was challenging and hard for her.

These sorts of lessons will show up in your career and business endeavors time and time again. The choice is yours: will you embrace them with grit and grace, or give up? I promise, if you don't crumble under your perceived limitations, you will eventually see the fruits of your labor! Focus on progress (not perfection), persevere, and find joy in every endeavor. This is the Divine Feminine flowing through you!

There will always be a necessary dance of Divine Feminine and Masculine energies in business. The Divine Feminine is all about surrender, creativity, trusting Divine timing, being in flow, allowing ourselves to be guided, and releasing control. The Divine Masculine is about positive self-discipline, action, having plans, setting goals, and building systems. When you allow both energies to work together, your career/business will thrive.* Have faith that your inner goddess knows what you need (and don't forget you can also follow the moon's and/or your menstrual cycle to really maximize your efforts!).

*FOOTNOTE: For example, while writing this book, I have been in peak flow. I've been waking up at 5 a.m. and writing/editing all day, every day, with ease and joy. Things have been going so smoothly, in fact, that my health and wellness business has started to explode with momentum! For awhile, I actually set this book aside because my goddess told me I should focus all of my energy and efforts on my business (and I figured I would probably learn some valuable lessons to include here!). Instead of forcing myself to continue writing, I trusted my goddess and my intuition and allowed my attention to flow where needed. Within those few months, I earned a promotion and my business exploded. As you can see, I eventually returned to the book when I felt inspired to keep writing!

It took me a long time to understand this dance. For seven years in my business, I combatted every limiting belief and behavioral pattern you can imagine. I would get trapped in a fixed mindset, desperate to reprogram negative thoughts. I thought I had to struggle to be successful and that titles and paychecks reflected my worthiness. I knew deep down within me there was a powerful goddess who could create amazing things, but I was limited by the illusion of "hustle mode." I tried to force things, and ran my business from a place of need and lack, not abundance and growth. My actions weren't energetically aligned with what I really wanted, so it was hard to see any magic in what I was doing.

I remember the moment when I realized how out of balance my Divine Masculine and Feminine were in my business. I was a few months pregnant, Dylan and I were newly married, and we had just gotten an apartment in Ottawa that cost about as much as we were making. We needed to work our businesses more than ever—it was time to hustle! Logic made me think we needed to talk to anyone and everyone about our businesses, but Dylan felt differently. I'll never forget what he said to me: "I am only going to work with people who inspire me. I want to intentionally look for people who get me excited, who I want to talk to and learn from. Like a true partnership, so we can teach each other things and inspire each other." I knew he was right. We had to trust in the Universe's Divine timing and work hard, not act in desperation or try to force anything.

We sat down and wrote out descriptions of the types of dream partners we wanted to attract to our businesses. We knew we were looking for individuals who would be open and inspired. We described where they lived, what they looked like, and what their passions were. Within about two weeks, Dylan met a girl online who was almost exactly like the description he'd written out. In partnership with her, his business became more exciting and grew like it never had before. She also became our soul sister, and the three of us will be life-long friends.

A few months later, I had a similar experience. I was on Instagram and came across an amazing woman who inspired me so much. I had a powerful knowing we were meant to work together. I reached out to her, told her how much I admired and wanted to work with her, and she agreed to meet with me. At nine months pregnant, I sat on my couch and chatted with this incredible human. She was also pregnant with her first child, and had been manifesting a way to work from home before her baby was born. We were complete strangers but after connecting for two hours, we discovered how much we had in common. We agreed that Divine timing had brought us together! For months we talked and planned, until we were finally able to meet in person. The connection we'd shared virtually was just as powerful, if not more so, in person. She was exactly the kind of business partner, friend, and soul sister I'd been looking for months earlier. She joined my business and ran with it.

Within a year and a half, I experienced a powerful shift. I was working hard, but was so aligned that it didn't *feel* difficult. Every night, I prayed for and visualized my dream life. Every morning, I awoke with purpose and passion. I had crystal clear vision; I knew what I wanted and where my business partners and I were going. I got very serious about my spiritual connection and raising my vibration. I spoke with the voice of my inner goddess, and saw the god or goddess in every person with whom I interacted. It flowed so magically and virtually everyone to whom I spoke would say they'd been looking for exactly what I was offering. It was exhilarating and exciting! As a team, we began to generate more earnings than ever before (we increased our sales volume by 600%!) and helped hundreds of people awaken to their potential, improve their lifestyle, and change their lives. Together we continue to attract other amazing humans who want to grow and help others; fellow gods and goddesses who are totally aligned with our personal values and business ethics.

This New Age of Business is a beautiful alignment of abundance and service. I aim to connect and serve, instead of forcing a sale. My goal always is, "How can I help this person?" My intention in business is first to connect to my spirituality and *then* do my work through it. When we have a spiritual relationship with God, our *Dea*, the Universe, or our higher self (whatever resonates with you), we usually leave it at the door when we get to work. We disconnect from our intuitive nature and plug into our job, like robots on an assembly line, but this is not sustainable if we want to live enriched, fulfilled lives. When we enjoy what we do, and follow a higher purpose, we can serve the world better. If you don't love what you're doing, go back to the human needs and see if you can find a way to enjoy and appreciate the work you're doing now. If not, practice gratitude for it anyway because it's providing you income and stability, while also showing you what you *don't* want; then use this as a guideline to discover your true passion. Fill the hours outside of work with activities you enjoy, and surround yourself with people who uplift and inspire you. There is so much opportunity for you out there—the possibilities are endless!

Imagine: a world in which everyone goes to work feeling alive, inspired, and excited about their days; a global movement where we collaborate to improve our companies, products, and services; a collective mission to help more people and heal the planet; and a universal culture in which it is safe, even encouraged, to try new things, regardless if you fail. How would *you* feel if you woke up feeling excited and passionate about what you were going to do that day? What if you had such strong faith in your business that you knew everything was working out for you exactly as it should? What if you could work from anywhere? What if you were being celebrated for every achievement, great and small, and instead of being envious of others, you celebrated their successes too? Can you visualize operating from a place of spiritual connection, in partnership with your *Dea*?

The *Dea* is calling for us to awaken to our own inner power and bring our Divine Feminine energy to the business world. If we can release our egos and operate from our souls, this work will be more harmonious, peaceful, expansive, and inclusive. The Divine Feminine is empathetic and compassionate, without greed or hoarding of resources. Corruption cannot live where the Divine Feminine thrives. The more open we are to this paradigm shift, the more harmonious and abundant the world will become.

The New Age of Business is about setting intentions to serve and connect without having to convince or resort to pushy sales tactics. Customers/clients/consumers are craving authenticity and deep connection. They want to do business with people who are passionate, energetic, and vibrant. People want to be part of something greater than themselves. They want to be part of a movement, a community filled with deep fulfillment, upliftment, and purpose.

When you show up fully, shining your brilliant light, you will feel your Divine power and never again doubt your worth. The magic in your business/career will flow when you stop pushing and are confident you have what people are looking for. Aim for spiritual success, and financial success will follow. Be an example of what is possible for others by diving into your deep soul work. Inspire those around you to live higher and choose to be better, in business *and* in life.

SOUL WORK

We all have the same twenty-four hours in a day, so . . . how are you spending yours?

Figure out what your professional/business dreams are and get crystal clear on what it will take to build them.

Stop making to-do lists and actually schedule your priorities into your days and weeks. There are so many different planners, virtual or paper, that can make your life easier. Figure out what works best for you, and get to it! Be in integrity with yourself after you schedule something, too. Honor the hours you set to do your work by making them non-negotiable.

Even if you are currently in a job you don't love, can you find an hour or two every day to work on your passion? I assure you, you can. Look at how much time you spend on your phone (some have screen time features that will tell you exactly how long you're spending in each app). Could you reduce the amount of time you spend scrolling on social media or watching TV and get to work on what ignites your passion?

If you are a rare unicorn who isn't addicted to your phone or TV, ask yourself what other steps you could take to schedule your priorities better. If appropriate, ask your boss if you can work from home once a week to spare yourself some commuting time. Make a meal plan with your partner so you aren't cooking every night. Wake up an hour earlier to do your side hustle/soul work before your day job. There are so many ways to build your dreams while you're doing what's necessary to make ends meet.

You do not have to have several consecutive hours to build a powerful routine and accomplish big goals. Find the nooks and crannies in your day and commit to building your dreams in them. You may find fifteen minutes here, a half hour there, a ten-minute break in the afternoon . . . get creative, and you'll be astonished at what you can accomplish.

When it comes time to work, create a routine that inspires you to stay on task. In order to write this book, I wake up at 5 or 6 a.m. every day so I have about an hour to myself before my husband and daughter wake up. I listen to meditation music, diffuse essential oils, drink a large bottle of water, connect with my *Dea*, and then get to writing. This routine puts me in a great mood, fills me with energy, and starts my day off right. I love this new habit because once

I'm done with this book, I'll be able to apply it to other work and creative projects, or activities like yoga, reading, meditation, gratitude practice, and more.

Share your experience online with #IdeaSoulWork.

Chapter 17

Sisterhood

A few months after I started my health and wellness business, I attended my first conference in Niagara Falls. I was still so new and didn't know what to expect. I didn't know much about the company culture yet, and was terrified I wouldn't be accepted or liked by the other consultants. I'd always had a tough time bonding with other girls, convinced women only ever competed with and judged one another. Little did I know that at that first conference, I would be introduced to my new family. Instead of stepping into a "sales convention" with 1,100 catty, competitive consultants, I was immersed in a vibrant community of positive, supportive soul sisters. Women who were basically total strangers would approach me and ask friendly questions, tell me how awesome my life was going to be, and give me advice. I left that conference more inspired than ever, blown away by how genuine, empowering, and kind everyone was. At nineteen years old, I'd finally discovered the true meaning of Sisterhood.

Female friendships had always been complicated for me. When I was twelve years old, my "best friend" bullied me mercilessly. She deliberately embarrassed me in front of our classmates and friends and said mean things about me, both to my face and behind my back. I was only in sixth grade, but people were already spreading rumors about and judging me, for no reason at all. They teased me about my clothes and appearance, and then in high school made fun of me for not wanting to drink or do drugs. I started to believe my only line of defense was to join in. Hoping to deflect the negative attention from myself, I projected it onto others and engaged in ugly, cruel gossip. I watched the girls around me transform from vicious rumormongers to sweet-faced imposters, depending on whom they were around, and resigned myself to the fact that girls were incapable of being honest with and nice to each other.

I was trapped in a web of deceit, backstabbing, and two-faced "friendships." It felt like the only way to survive. I couldn't understand why we thought it was okay to disparage other people and their lives, where they lived and worked, how they dressed, etc. but I was afraid if I didn't participate, I would go back to being the subject of their ridicule (of course, I now realize if they gossiped *with* me, they were definitely gossiping *about* me). I convinced myself I wasn't the problem; the other girls were. I was "just trying to get by" and blamed them for forcing me to become a mean girl like them. I resented them when they made me feel bad, and loved them when they included me. It was a toxic cycle that I now understand wasn't friendship at all (and it most certainly wasn't Sisterhood).

"Comparison is the thief of joy." - Theodore Roosevelt

Self-judgement can lead to brutal comparisons and competition with others, especially between women. Magazines, television, movies, and fashion have always promoted unrealistic beauty standards and unhealthy comparisons—and social media has only exacerbated the problem. Every day we are confronted with posts and images that *we* allow to make us feel inadequate. But why? Why are we so afraid of being judged? Why are we so scared to show our true selves to the world? Why do we put ourselves down, shrink away from our greatness, and stay curled up in our comfort zones?

I've learned over the years that hurt people hurt people. I've realized when we fear judgement from others, it's because *we* judge others. It seems harsh, but it's true. If you didn't judge people for their decisions, actions, and beliefs, then it wouldn't cross your mind that you could be judged for your own (sit with that for a moment). We all do it, so don't beat yourself up, but evaluate what bothers you about other people and then look *inward*. People are mirroring back to us what we love and dislike about ourselves, and with more awareness, we can reprogram these thoughts and behaviors.

Even if we can't recognize ourselves in our judgements of others, we *can* work on having more empathy for people who are different than us. Chances are good, you have been the victim of gossip at some point; did it feel good? Of course not. We have to remember the old adages: "walk a mile in someone else's shoes;" "treat others how you want to be treated;" and "if you don't have something nice to say, don't say anything at all."

Humanity is broken right now, in need of deep, soulful healing. Though there are beautiful differences amongst us that should be celebrated, we all have the same color of blood running through our veins and share the same basic structural makeup. We've all experienced love, been hurt, felt sad, and been happy. And we are all connected by pure, Divine energy. When we make a conscious decision to love, respect, and appreciate ourselves, and then treat every human being with respect, gratitude, and love, no matter how "different" they may seem, the healing process can begin.

Your *Dea* wants you to shine in all your Divine glory, goddess. One of the best ways to feel truly positive and uplifted, grow your self-confidence, and get inspired is to spread positivity, uplift other women, compliment and praise fellow goddesses, and inspire people with your own personal growth journey. Recognize and honor the potential in everyone: their power, light, love, and uniqueness. Celebrate another woman's beauty on social media instead of quietly judging or comparing yourself to her. When a friend launches a new business, cheer for her more loudly than anyone else and ask how you can help. Broadcast your sisters' accomplishments to the world and say how proud you are of them. As Bob Goff (Lawyer, Speaker, Author) says, "Throw kindness around like confetti." Compliment *everyone*. Make a firm decision to stop gossiping. Treat every woman (*including yourself!*) as if she were your best friend or sister.

Divine Friendships

Sisterhood is available to us in many different ways. Sometimes we are born into it; other times, we find our life-long best friends as young children; and occasionally, we don't find our closest, most precious goddess girlfriends until we are well into adulthood. I have been blessed with many different female friendships throughout my life, but my relationship with my sister Aya has always been my most cherished; it has also always been the benchmark for my relationships with other women.

Aya and I are sisters *and* best friends. We've grown up together, of course, but we've also grown as women alongside each other because we challenge each other to always be and do better. We hold one another to high standards, and never allow each other to settle for less than we deserve. Aya and I remind each other who we truly are when we cannot see it ourselves. We are there for each other when one of us needs a shoulder to cry on, but we don't let each other fall into victimhood. We speak life and love over each other in good and hard times.

This is what all Sisterhood should be: a safe space where you can share how you feel without judgement; where you seek to understand and listen, as well as be understood and heard; where you unconditionally support your fellow goddesses through joy and sorrow; and where you openly and honestly communicate, even when it's difficult. True Sisterhood is about loving, accepting, and honoring your sisters wherever they're at in their journeys. It's about transcending the juvenile middle and high school days of gossip, popularity contests, and unnecessary drama. In a Divine friendship, you exchange expectations for edification and gratitude.

Sisterhood is about affirming your friends. When your friend needs a positive reminder, tell her, "You got this! You work so hard! You deserve the best! You are a brilliant freaking goddess and nothing can stop you from having the most amazing life!" Don't compare, criticize, or condemn. But it is also about being brave enough to have tough conversations. Sometimes Sisterhood requires us to share the hard truth. When a soul sister is making destructive choices, you and your *Dea* may need to show up with some tough love. We must be mindful not to further enable bad situations, but rather empower our friends to make strong choices that align with their Divine power. Instead of injecting more negativity into situations, do your very best to gently and objectively guide your friends through their feelings so they can forgive, heal, and grow. And of course, we must be open to receiving and hearing these hard truths, too!

I absolutely love and honor my soul sisters who show up in friendship with Divine understanding and pure love in their hearts. My best friends are so special because we can live our own lives and not see each other or even speak for months without resentment. When we do get together or catch up, we pick up right where we left off, as if we had just spoken the day before. My Divine friendships are filled with love, honor, and acceptance instead of expectations, codependency, and drama. And when things get rocky (because no one is perfect) we trust each other enough to be open and honest, and receptive to constructive feedback.

In order to restore the Divine Feminine to the world, we must restore it within ourselves and our relationships with each other. There is nothing more powerful than Sisters united on a mission, awakened goddesses shining brightly and rising together. My fellow goddesses, let's start a movement to consciously and lovingly spread Sisterhood (Brotherhood/Humanhood) across the globe to *all* humans.

SOUL WORK

I challenge you to put down this book and send messages of love and encouragement to five (or more!) sacred Sisters. They could be your sister, mother/maternal figure, close friends, business partners, mentor, cousins, online friends, or even total strangers on social media!

Make it your mission to spread "sisterly love" as much as possible and see how it makes you feel. Turn your home, work/business environments, friend circles, and social media accounts into positive, loving, accepting, equitable, inclusive, and uplifting places, free from drama and negativity.

Share your experience online with #IdeaSoulWork.

Chapter 18

Surrender

The other day, my two-year-old daughter was frustrated and started yelling, clearly desperate to release the big ball of feelings boiling up inside of her. Normally I would have tried to show her how to calm her emotions, but in that moment, I realized I could actually learn something from her. Because she allowed herself to feel *everything* and then release it all, she quickly went from yelling to smiling. She didn't fight or suppress what she was feeling, but resigned herself to the experience. I started saying, "YES! Get it out, baby!" She yelled some more, and then broke into a huge grin. My husband, who had come into the room to make sure we were okay, grabbed a pillow from the couch and we all took turns screaming into it. The frustration our toddler had been feeling became an opportunity for all of us to just *let sh** go.* Eventually the three of us erupted in laughter, giggling at how silly we were being. The lesson our funny little girl taught us that day was: *surrender.*

Too many of us stifle our emotions and fight against them, instead of leaning into and surrendering to them. When we do this, they typically manifest within our bodies as dis-ease and disharmony. I highly recommend learning how to surrender to and process your feelings instead of bottling them up so much that you either get sick or explode in anger. Laugh maniacally, jump up and down, go for a run, howl at the moon, or yell into a pillow—I promise you'll feel better, and be better for it!

Surrender is often associated with giving up and being defeated. That's not what I mean. Emotional, energetic surrender is about releasing our human attachment to and control over how we think things need to happen. Surrender allows us to feel more elated and free, to have faith and trust in a greater power beyond ourselves. When we surrender, we connect to our intuition and the flow of the Universe. True surrender means we have found a balance between our Divine Masculine (setting goals and intentions and then meeting the Universe halfway with inspired action) and our Divine Feminine (trusting and flowing with our inner goddesses).

I have had to learn how to surrender over and over . . . and over again. Remember when I visited Dylan and when he picked me up from the airport, he told me he'd met his soulmate? That entire experience was a lesson in surrender, but there's even more to the story.

The week before I flew to Kansas, I was in New York City on a business trip with a soul sister of mine. One afternoon, she and I had a meeting at a quaint restaurant on a boat on the Hudson River. I was sitting at the bar, sipping on a lemonade, when I noticed a man staring at me. He was attractive and intriguing; I felt a strong pull between us. It wasn't like the soul connection I had with Dylan, but there was definitely a strong magnetism between us—and it confused the hell out of me! I was going to Kansas the next day to find out if Dylan was "The One," and yet I found myself very physically attracted to this man. Within a few minutes, he confidently walked over, flirted, and bought me another lemonade. We talked for about thirty minutes about all sorts of things: business, travel, the Law of Attraction, health and wellness, and more. He seemed like an incredible person. Before he left, we exchanged numbers and he gave me a kiss on the cheek. I was stunned and completely baffled. *Why would I meet this amazing guy right before I'm going to solidify things with Dylan?! What is this, Universe? What is happening?! I'm so confused. What should I do? What is the lesson here?! I thought Dylan was The One. Is he not? Is this testing my resolve, making sure I'm really committed to him?*

My friend and I went to the end of the pier so we could talk and hopefully help me clear my mind. I watched the waves of the Hudson, feeling confused and frustrated. I needed to figure out how to regain control of the situation and, more importantly, my thoughts and feelings! Finally, I threw my hands up in the air and said, "Why am I trying to figure this out?! I know the Universe has my back, and it knows how everything is meant to play out. I trust that whatever is meant to be, will be, so I'm just going to go on this wild ride. I surrender." In that moment, I felt blissful joy and peaceful release.

And then I heard the beautiful young girl sitting next to me ask, "Will you take a picture of me?"

I looked over to respond and realized . . . she hadn't actually said anything! She was staring out at the water, with her phone in her hand. *What is going on?* I thought. I decided to check in with her, just in case. "Hey, do you want me to take a picture of you?"

She looked at me in shock. "I *just* thought about asking you in my head! But I thought it would be weird to ask you girls."

"Well I heard you! And it's totally not weird. You look too gorgeous in this scene not to have a photo!" I took a few pictures of her and the three of us ended up chatting, which led to getting dinner and spending the entire evening hanging out together. We had so much in common—our new friend was also vegan and into the Law of Attraction and wellness. We laughed, cried, shared secrets, and opened up about past wounds. The connection the three of us shared was unreal—instantaneous Sisterhood.

That night, as I fell asleep, I realized it had been a day of Divine guidance and learning how to let go. The moment I decided to surrender, and release the confusion I was feeling about Dylan, my *Dea* introduced me to this wonderful new soul sister.

Things got even clearer when I arrived in Kansas and Dylan told me about his "soulmate." I knew I had met the man on the boat so I wouldn't crumble when I heard Dylan's news. The Universe wanted me to see that I didn't have to be so attached to a future with Dylan; that I could connect with other people too. The Divine orchestrated the whole thing to help me surrender, stay in my faith, and refrain from my human masculine need to control everything. I had to lean into my Divine Feminine and let things flow. This helped me feel more comfortable being myself around Dylan, which allowed him to get to know the *real* me during that trip (and the rest, as they say, is history!).

My other BIG lesson in surrender came when I was pregnant. That experience forced me to release control and fully trust in a totally foreign process I'd never been through before. I had absolutely no power over having morning sickness, or when contractions would start, or how long delivery would take. After she was born, I couldn't dictate when my baby would sleep, or how long she'd sleep, if she'd breastfeed well, or how my body would feel recovering from childbirth. It was the ultimate surrender, and I grew *a lot* through it.

Now, as I wrap up this book, I am pregnant with my second baby girl and though my first trimester started the same (extreme sickness to the point of needing anti-nausea medication), I have felt calmer and at peace. I am consciously choosing to heal my past traumas, surrender to the process, and welcome in a whole new experience. As a result, it has been so much more enjoyable! Dylan and I feel closer than ever because we worked on healing the past issues with intimacy that resulted from my first pregnancy. I am grateful for my magical body and trust my *Dea* to guide us through our next labor experience.

Surrender is so important to having a growth mindset and being open to the possibilities of the Divine. You do not need to have everything figured out all the time. Instead, trust the wisdom of your inner goddess and know she is taking you on the most amazing journey of self-discovery. Plant seeds of intention, water them with inspired action, and then surrender to the sunshine of the Universe.

The truth is, goddess, there is no ultimate destination. We never fully arrive, so stop limiting yourself with expectations over which you have zero control and open yourself up to the wonders of the Universe by turning inward. Gautama Buddha taught that the root of all human suffering is attachment. No person, amount of money, house, car, or material thing outside of you can fulfill you or make you happy. The only thing that can make you truly happy and joyful is your connection to your inner Divinity. We are here to expand, evolve, and experience new things; to have limitless desires and create everything we dream of. But in order to achieve our big dreams, we have to detach from the outcome and surrender to the process. What is meant to be, will be. It may feel like you're falling backward off a cliff sometimes, like a "trust fall" into the clouds, but know that your *Dea* is by your side, building your wings and helping you fly.

Right now, in this very moment, you can choose to make your life more magical than you've ever imagined. Trust and listen to your inner goddess. The *Dea* is yearning for you to awaken her so she can bring you the most harmonious, flowing, abundant, powerful life filled with Love.

SOUL WORK

If you are ready to surrender and call Her in, to receive and welcome in your greatness, I invite you to incorporate these mantras into your life.

I, *Dea*, am powerful beyond measure and capable of creating anything I desire.

I, *Dea*, am filled with infinite light and love that overflows to the world around me.

I, *Dea*, am at your disposal to co-create magic beyond our wildest dreams.

I, *Dea*, am vibrant and healthy, and am filled with vitality and magnetic charisma.

I, *Dea*, am the source of abundance that is always flowing to me.

I, *Dea*, am infinitely worthy of unconditional love and passion.

I, *Dea*, am you, and you, *Dea*, are me.

Chapter 19

The Rise of the Feminine

Awaken Her in you. Awaken Her to the world.

Let's begin . . .

Sources and References

1. Retrieved from an audio dictation by Mother Hamilton. Accessed January 5, 2020. https://www.crossandlotus.com/Masters/mother_hamilton.html.

2. Byrne, Rhonda. 2006. *The Secret.* Accessed February 11, 2020. www.thesecret.tv.

3. Abraham Hicks Publications. Accessed February 14, 2020. https://www.abraham-hicks.com.

4. All That's Interesting. 2015. "The Historical Origins of the Witch." Last modified Sept. 17, 2020. https://allthatsinteresting.com/history-of-witches.

5. History.com. 2017. "History of Witches." Last modified Feb. 21, 2020. https://www.history.com/topics/folklore/history-of-witches.

6. History.com. 2017. "Christianity." Last modified Oct. 8, 2019. https://www.history.com/topics/religion/history-of-christianity.

7. Lee, Jennie. 2019. "What Is the True Meaning of Yoga?." www.yogapedia.com/what-is-the-true-meaning-of-yoga/2/9038.

8. Gaia. 2017. Yogic Paths - Season 1, Episode 4. "Tantra: The Householders's Path." Accessed April 2, 2020. https://www.gaia.com/series/yogic-paths.

9. Chopra.com. 2016. "Shakti: A Universal Force." https://chopra.com/article/shakti-universal-force.

10. Britannica. 1998. "*Tara.*" Last modified October 31, 2017. https://www.britannica.com/topic/Tara-Buddhist-goddess.

11. Wicca Living. *n.d.* "A Brief Summary of Core Wiccan Beliefs." Accessed April 20, 2020. https://wiccaliving.com/essentials-wicca/.

12. Elliot, Candice. 2020. "The Pink Tax: What's the Cost of Being a Female Consumer in 2020?." Accessed September 12, 2020. https://www.listenmoneymatters.com/the-pink-tax/.

13. Emoto, Masaru. Accessed May 12, 2020. www.masaru-emoto.net

14. IKEA UAE. 2018. "Bully A Plant: Say No to Bullying." Youtube, April 30, 2018. https://www.youtube.com/watch?v=Yx6UgfQreYY.

15. Access Consciousness. Accessed May 30, 2020. www.accessconsciousness.com

16. Cartwright, Marc. 2016. "Atlantis." Accessed June 4, 2020. www.ancient.eu/atlantis.

17. Robbins, Tony. *n.d.* "6 Human Needs: Do You Need to Feel Significant?" Accessed June 25, 2020. www.tonyrobbins.com/mind-meaning/do-you-need-to-feel-significant.

18. Isabel, Maria. 2018. "The Sacred Role of Menstrual Blood in Native American Culture." Accessed June 26, 2020. www.culturacolectiva.com/history/menstruation-sacred-role-for-native-americans.

19. Vaughn, Emily. 2019. "Menstrual Huts Are Illegal in Nepal. So Why Are Women Still Dying in Them?" Accessed June 28, 2020. www.npr.org/sections/goatsandsoda/2019/12/17/787808530/menstrual-huts-are-illegal-in-nepal-so-why-are-women-still-dying-in-them.

20. Press Release from Wired Release. 2020. "Feminine Hygiene Products Market Report 2020 Share, Size, Trends, Forecast and Analysis of Key Players 2025." Accessed October 10, 2020. https://apnews.com/5966bd78d30b05c6a4faaa73a56c342a#:~:text=in%20its%20creation.-,Feminine%20Hygiene%20Products%20Market%20Report%202020%20Share%2C%20Size%2C%20Trends%2C,Analysis%20of%20Key%20players%202025&text=Sheridan%2C%20Wyoming%2C%20USA%2C%20March,US%24%2026.0%20Billion%20in%202019.

21. Fourth Trimester Collective- Community Organization. 2020. Accessed June 30, 2020. www.facebook.com/fourthtrimestercollective.

22. Thomashauer, Regena. 2016. *Pussy: A Reclamation.* Hay House, Inc.

23. Chapman, Gary. 1992. *The 5 Love Languages: The Secret to Love That Lasts.* Northfield Publishing.

24. Montgomery, Heather. 2018. "How Often Do 'Normal' Couples Have Sex?" Accessed June 10, 2020. https://www.healthline.com/health/baby/how-often-do-normal-couples-have-sex#The-Average.

25. Cherry, Kendra. 2020. "The 4 Major Jungian Archetypes. "Accessed October 13, 2020. www.verywellmind.com/what-are-jungs-4-major-archetypes-2795439

26. Canfield, Jack and Janet Switzer. 2006. *The Success Principles™.* William Morrow Paperbacks.

27. Dyer, Wayne. *n.d.* "Success Secrets." Accessed July 2, 2020. www.drwaynedyer.com/blog/success-secrets.

28. Dispenza, Dr. Joe. 2012. *Breaking the Habit of Being Yourself: How to Lose Your Mind and Create a New One.* Hay House Inc.

29. Dispenza, Dr. Joe. 2012. *Breaking the Habit of Being Yourself: How to Lose Your Mind and Create a New One.* Hay House Inc.

30. Dispenza, Dr. Joe. Meditations. www.drjoedispenza.com/collections/meditations-english.

31. Hinchliffe, Emma. 2020. "The number of female CEOs in the Fortune 500 hits an all-time record." Accessed July 17, 2020. https://fortune.com/2020/05/18/women-ceos-fortune-500-2020.

32. Desilver, Drew. 2015. "A Record Number of Women Will be Serving in 116th Congress." Last modified December 18, 2018. https://www.pewresearch.org/fact-tank/2018/12/18/record-number-women-in-congress/.

33. Opfer, Chris. 2019. "Henry Ford vs. the Dodge Brothers: An All-American Feud." Accessed July 24, 2020. https://auto.howstuffworks.com/henry-ford-vs-dodge-brothers-all-american-feud.htm.

34. Freidman, Zach. 2019. "78% Of Workers Live Paycheck to Paycheck." Accessed August 8, 2020. www.forbes.com/sites/zackfriedman/2019/01/11/live-paycheck-to-paycheck-government-shutdown/#696db44e4f10.

35. Dweck, Carol. 2014. "The Power of Believing you can Improve." Filmed September, 2014 in Norrköping, Sweden. TED video, 10:13. www.ted.com/talks/carol_dweck_the_power_of_believing_that_you_can_improve/discussion.

Made in the USA
Monee, IL
04 November 2020